One more step

Assemblies for secondary schools (Pupils aged 11–15)

W J WILCOCK

SIMON & SCHUSTER
EDUCATION

To Zoë Rachael

First published in 1993 in the United Kingdom by
Simon & Schuster Education
Campus 400, Maylands Avenue
Hemel Hempstead, Herts HP2 7EZ

British Library Cataloguing in Publication Data is
available on request from the British Library

ISBN 0 7501 0521 6

Printed in Great Britain by Hartnoll Bound, Cornwall.

Contents

Spring term

Summer term

Foreword

The 1988 Education Act requires all state schools to provide a daily act of worship which is mainly of a Christian nature. This assembly book should prove a valuable resource, filling the requirements of the Education Act. The format, being similar to that of my first book, *Through the year*, published in 1990, provides for one assembly a week for two complete years, the themes being linked to both the Christian calendar and the academic year.

Although intended for pupils in secondary schools to the age of 15, the themes could easily be adapted for use with older or indeed much younger pupils. Most of the themes are suitable for use in multi-faith situations, but in each case there is a conclusion which brings out some aspect of the Christian faith.

In compiling my books I have drawn upon thirty-five years of teaching experience, in latter years as Head of Lower School, and my experience as a lay preacher in churches of many denominations. Since my recent retirement from education I have kept very much in touch with the needs of colleagues in my capacity as a member of the local Standing Advisory Council for Religious Education.

The prayer at the end of each assembly refers to a numbered prayer in the *Prayer* section towards the end of the book.

W J Wilcock

Acknowledgements

The author and publisher would like to thank the following for permission to reproduce copyright material:

Extracts from *The Guinness Book of Records 1993* Copyright © Guinness Publishing Ltd 1992; 'Diary of a Church Mouse' from *Collected Poems of John Betjeman*, John Murray (Publishers) Ltd; St John Ambulance; Arsenal Football Club; Aston Villa Football Club; Everton Football Club; Liverpool Football Club; Manchester City Football Club; Nottingham Forest Football Club; Tottenham Hotspur Football Club; Scripture Union; Gideons International; A & C Black Ltd (publishers of Who's Who); The Ministry of Defence; Extracts from 'The Return of Heroic Failures' by Stephen Pile, reprinted by permission of Martin Secker and Warburg Ltd.

Every effort has been made to trace all the copyright holders, but if any have been inadvertently overlooked, the publishers would be pleased to hear from them.

Year 1
Autumn term

Tracks

Week 1

Introduction	Welcome to a new school or new year-group
Aim	To show that we all leave our mark upon the world
Visual Aids	Cards showing tracks (see overleaf)

Our theme today is 'making our mark'. Without realising it, we leave evidence of our presence wherever we have been. Many of you will have visited the seaside recently and will no doubt have left footprints in the sand. These would be very noticeable if the tide had just gone out and you were the first to walk on the 'new' sand.

See if you can guess what or who has made these tracks. (*Show the cards and invite suggestions.*)

Answers:
1 A person on roller skates.
2 A child on a scooter.
3 A person wheeling two bicycles.
4 A person walking on their hands.
5 Children in a wheelbarrow race.
6 Children in a three-legged race.

Everywhere we go we leave our mark. Some leave a trail of destruction! Has your mother ever said to you 'Please tidy your bedroom, it looks as though a bomb has dropped on it'?

In history and science lessons we learn of the achievements of great scholars and leaders who have left their mark upon the world. Sportsmen and women regularly perform outstanding feats which are recorded for posterity. By comparison you may feel there isn't much you can do to make your mark. Everyone here will make his or her mark upon the life of our school during the year that lies ahead and I assure you that your work, behaviour and contributions to the life of the school will all be noticed. I hope the mark you're going to make will be a good one.

Christian application

The followers of Jesus Christ have all been given different talents to use in his service. How marvellous that even ordinary people such as ourselves can be used by him to bring the good news of his love to the world.

Our reading lists some of these talents but not all by any means.

Reading Romans 12, 6–10

In our new school we must try to develop our God-given talents. We do this when we are helpful, caring and kind. These are the best kinds of marks to leave on our school.

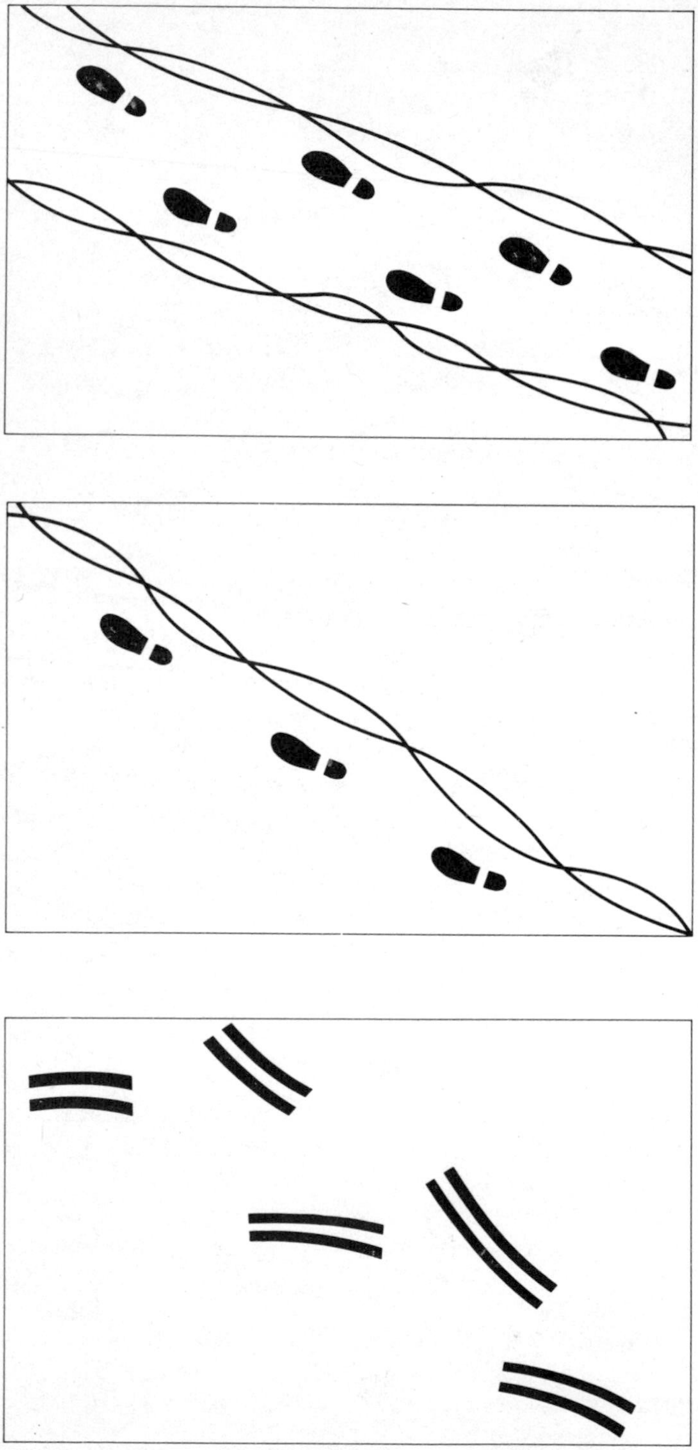

Track 3

Track 2

Track 1

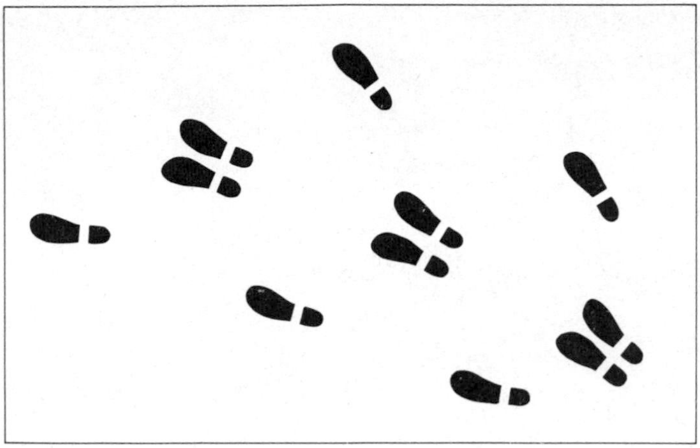

Track 6

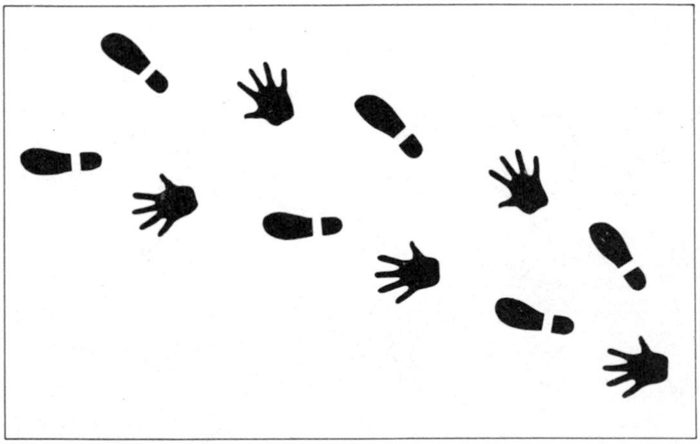

Track 5

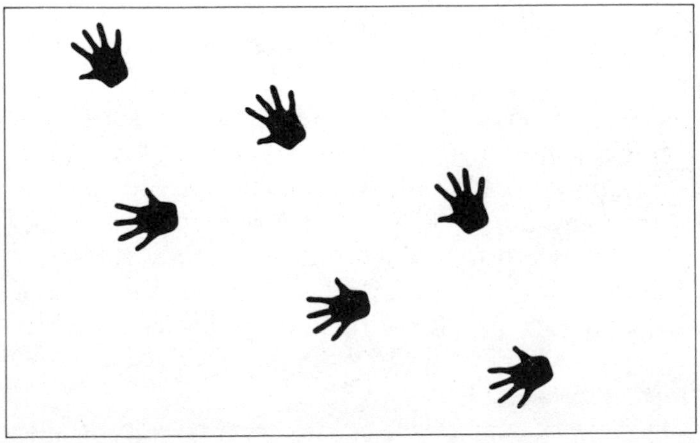

Track 4

You are writing a gospel
A chapter each day,
By the deeds that you do
And the words that you say.
Men read what you write
Whether faithless or true.
Say, what is the gospel
According to *YOU*?

Prayer No 45
Hymn 'One more step along the world I go'
'Forth in thy name O Lord I go'

Stumped

Week 2

Aim To help pupils to settle into their new school/year group/class
Visual Aid A fiftieth birthday card

It was Grandad's fiftieth birthday. Knowing that his Grandad was a keen cricket follower, Sanjit sent him a card like this with the message 'Congratulations, Grandad, you are fifty not out'.

The cricket season has just drawn to a close, so I thought we would consider today some sayings which come from this game but which are now used in everyday conversation. Perhaps we shall be able to apply some of them to our life at school.

When a new batsman goes out to face the bowling he often takes a little time to play himself in, to get used to the bowling before attempting to score lots of runs. At present you are 'playing yourself in' – finding your bearings and getting used to new work and new teachers. Before long you should begin to feel confident and start to make good progress with your studies.

If often happens during a cricket match that there is a shower of rain followed by a bright sunny spell. These weather conditions affect the cricket wicket making it possible for the slow bowlers to spin the ball more. A batsman may thus find himself struggling on a 'sticky wicket'. Things only get difficult for us at school if we allow ourselves to be distracted from our work or if we become lazy or disobedient. It is then that we begin to find the work difficult because we are batting on a sticky wicket. We need never be in that predicament. All we have to do is try our best.

Back now to the game of cricket. There are several ways that a batsman can be out. One is to be stumped by the wicket keeper. It often happens that a batsman thinks the bowler has bowled an easy ball which can be hit to the boundary. He takes a stride down the wicket beyond his batting crease, but unfortunately he then misses the ball. This gives the wicket keeper the chance to catch the ball and whip off the bails. The batsman is given out by the umpire, 'stumped'.

People are sometimes said to be 'stumped for an answer' if they do not know what to say, if they do not understand the question or if they are having difficulty with the work. You need never be 'stumped', for your teachers are always willing to explain the work again to you if you will let them know you are in difficulty.

A cricket ball which is knocked clean over the boundary line without a bounce scores six runs. It has been 'hit for six'.

Should we think that things are getting on top of us, that our problems are too much to cope with it is sometimes said that we, like the cricket ball, have been 'hit for six'. If ever you feel like this, remember that your teacher or tutor will be very pleased to help you sort out your problems.

Christian application
If ever we feel stumped or hit for six we can of course ask our Heavenly Father to help because he promises to give us the strength we need to face every problem (see Romans 8, 28 and 2 Corinthians 12, 9).

Reading Proverbs 3, 1–6
Prayer No 24
Hymn 'Seek ye first the kingdom of God'

Tip

Week 3

Theme Faithfulness

Joseph Tagg was an old shepherd who had worked for many years on the Derbyshire hillsides near the Lady Bower reservoir. He had long since retired and now lived on his own, his only companion being a dog called Tip, his faithful sheepdog on whom he had relied so much during his working days. But they still went for frequent walks up into the hills he loved so much. One day in 1953 they set off as usual, but Joe was never seen alive again. When Joe and Tip did not return, neighbours organised a search party but all they could find was Joe's cap up on the mountain side. It was some three months later that a group of shepherds found Joe's body on the hillside where he had died. There beside the body was faithful Tip, a handful of skin and bone but still alive, standing broken-hearted by his master. Tip had brought bones to feed him and had stayed alive by feeding on dead birds.

When Tip eventually died the villagers organised a public subscription to raise a memorial to the dog, man's best friend. The memorial read as follows:

IN
COMMEMORATION OF
THE DEVOTION OF
TIP
THE SHEEPDOG WHICH STAYED
BY THE BODY OF HIS DEAD
MASTER MR. JOSEPH TAGG ON
HOWDEN MOORS FOR FIFTEEN
WEEKS FROM 12th DECEMBER
1953 to 27th MARCH 1954

What a marvellous example of faithfulness and loyalty. Can you think of ways in which we should be faithful?

Examples: Be faithful to our friends
Be faithful to our families
Be faithful to our school

Christian application

Reading Matthew 25, 14–40: parable of the talents
We could not possibly have any greater reward than to have the Lord say of us 'Well done thou good and faithful servant'.

Prayer No 8 and/or No 16

Hymns 'I have decided to follow Jesus'

Call my bluff

Week 4

Theme Deception

Visual Aids Two sheets with the words:

ABLEWHACKET

SPLAW

Today, with the help of some volunteers we are going to play a game known as *Call My Bluff*. Each pupil in turn will give you a definition of a word and then I will ask you to decide which is the correct meaning, for only one of the three is true.

1ST PUPIL: Ablewhacket is a card game, rather like whist, which was played by *able* seamen; that explains the first part of the word. The whacket bit comes in when one of the seamen loses. He has to hold out his hand so that the others can whack it!

2ND PUPIL: If you have ever been to Somerset for your holiday you may have heard the word Ablewhacket because it is to do with cider-making, for which that county is famous. When the apples are crushed in order to remove the juice so that the cider can be made, there is a lot of pulp left over. This isn't wasted. It is fed to the pigs. They love it. The pulp is called Ablewhacket.

3RD PUPIL: Of course the first two meanings are quite wrong. I will tell you the true meaning of Ablewhacket. If you started to shiver and sneeze and got runny eyes and a sore throat you would *not* have caught Ablewhacket, you would have caught a common cold. But if you were a chicken and had the same symptoms it certainly would be called Ablewhacket!

Now let's vote. How many think the true meaning was the first? The second? The third? Well! *Ablewhacket* was a card game played by seamen!

Here is another chance for you to guess right. The second word is **splaw**.

4TH PUPIL: A splaw is a large nail which railway workers used to secure the brackets holding railway lines to the wooden sleepers.

5TH PUPIL: Wrong! A splaw is a small copper coin in use in Scotland from 1450 until the Union of Scotland and England in 1603.

6TH PUPIL: Wrong again! Splaw is an adjective which describes someone who has two left feet and is always stumbling and walking into doors, etc.

(*Again take a vote*.)

When you leave this assembly take care not to be splaw. Someone who is *splaw* is clumsy!

How easily are you deceived? Take care not to be misled by advertisements. Be careful not to be taken in by those who say that you can be successful without hard work. Do not be influenced by those who tell you that it doesn't matter how you behave because you won't be found out. Don't be deceived.

Christian application

Although we are frequently misled or deceived by other people, there is someone who can never be deceived.

Reading	Galatians 6, 7–10
	God can never be deceived
Prayer	No 9 and/or No 35
Hymn	'Be bold, be strong'
	'I'm very glad of God'

Harvest time

Week 5

Aim	To show God's faithfulness and providence at harvest time
Visual Aid	A copy of *The Guinness Book of Records* and a large coconut

Here are some interesting facts from *The Guinness Book of Records*, all about seeds. Apparently, the smallest seed in the world is that of the epiphytic orchid which is so minute that there are 35,000,000 to the ounce; and the largest seed in the world is that of the double coconut which only grows in the Seychelles in the Indian Ocean. This seed weighs up to 44lbs (or 20kg). It is much larger than the one I have brought to show you. You will have learned in your biology lessons that all plants come from seeds. Now let me ask you a very difficult question: Which came first, the seed or the plant?

If you say 'the seed' then where did the seed come from? If you say the plant came first, then what did the plant grow from?

'Consider the lilies of the field how they grow,' said Jesus, who went on to explain that it is God who created them and provides such a beautiful array. (See Matthew 6, 28–30.)

This is the time of year when we thank God for the harvest, for giving life to the seeds and for sending the rain to help the seeds to grow and the sun to ripen the crops. In this way he shows his faithfulness and providence for humankind.

Christian application

Here is God's promise (read Genesis 8, 21 and 22): 'As long as earth remains, seed time and harvest shall not fail.'

God keeps his promise and provides sufficient food for everyone. The tragedy is that people have not yet learned how to share God's gifts with each other. Millions of people in Third World countries are starving, because the crops have failed again, or because their country is torn apart by war or simply because they do not have the technology to cultivate the land properly. Yet the nations which have plenty, and to spare, often seem reluctant to share.

Sadly, all too frequently, when aid is sent to stricken countries it is prevented from reaching its destination by the civil wars being waged in those countries.

This morning as we thank God for his plentiful harvest let us remember in our prayers all who are in desperate need.

Prayer No 21
Hymn 'Thank you for every new good morning'
'Colours of the day' (for younger pupils)

Murphy's law (and others) *Week 6*

Aim To show the sense and importance of God's laws

One day in 1949, at Edwards Air Force Base in California, research was being carried out on certain devices used in aircraft. When one particular device malfunctioned due to an error in the wiring, a development engineer named Captain Ed Murphy said in sheer exasperation: 'If there is anything which can possibly go wrong, it will!' This theory rapidly became known as *Murphy's Law* and is today widely quoted in all sorts of situations when things don't turn out as expected.

Here are some more so-called laws for you to consider (*Read out a selection from the following*):

O'Reilly's Law: No matter what goes wrong, there's always someone who knew it would.

Shanahan's Law: The length of the meeting is the square of the number of people present.

Parkinson's First Law: Work expands to fill the time available.

The First Law of Cycling: No matter which way you ride, it's uphill and against the wind.

Lewis's Law: No matter how long you shop for an item, after you have bought it you will see it on sale somewhere else – cheaper!

Simon's Law: Everything put together falls apart sooner or later.

Sodd's Second Law: Sooner or later the worst possible set of circumstances is bound to occur.

Scott's Law: No matter what goes wrong, it will probably look right!

Chisholm's Law: If things appear to be going well you have probably overlooked something.

Brennan's Law: Paper is always strongest at the perforations.

Dooley's Law: If something happens to you it will have already happened to your friends.

And – finally – *O'Toole's commentary on Murphy's Law*: Murphy was an optimist.

What did you make of those laws? You may have found some amusing, some rather cynical. Some you may not even have understood, but you will probably have experienced the truth of one or two of them yourself.

As we gain in experience and no doubt have difficulties to face, it is reassuring to know that others understand our problems; for they have had the same experiences.

Christian application

Here are some laws which are in no way cynical and which are perfectly clear to understand. They are God's laws.

Reading	Luke 10, 25–28. Love God with all your heart and your neighbour as yourself.
Prayer	No 22

Hymn 'Father lead me day by day'
'Let us with a gladsome mind'

Tom, Dick and Harry

Week 7

Aim To show that life has many mysteries
Visual Aid A card with the sums

$$3 \times 9 = 27$$

$$27 + 2 = 29$$

Tom, Dick and Harry worked for a local firm. They had all been given a rise; so they went out to celebrate. They decided to have a really good meal at a restaurant. The evening was most enjoyable and when it was time for them to leave they called the waiter and each gave him a ten pound note. (Meals were not as expensive in those days!) The waiter took the money over to the cashier who proceeded to work out the bill. It came in total to twenty five pounds so the cashier gave five one-pound coins in change to the waiter. Thinking that the three young men didn't look the sort who would give him a tip, the waiter, dishonestly, kept two pounds for himself and gave one pound change each to Tom, Dick and Harry. You will now be able to work out how much each paid for his meal. It was ten pounds less one pound, which comes to nine pounds each.

Here now is a problem for you to think about. Tom, Dick and Harry each paid nine pounds. Three times nine is twenty seven pounds. The waiter kept two pounds for himself. Twenty seven and two only adds up to twenty nine. What happened to the other pound?

You can discuss that at break later! If you think you have solved the mystery come and tell me – but please don't trouble your maths teachers. There is a trick in it – quite a mystery.

You will already be aware that life itself has many mysteries. In your studies you will learn the answers to many of life's mysteries. For example:

What causes an apple to fall from a tree to the ground?
Why does wood float in water but a piece of metal sinks?
What causes the tide to come in at the seaside?
Why is the sky blue?
How do we get a picture on our television?

Solving mysteries is what education is about. It can be very exciting.

Christian application
There are many mysteries for which we cannot readily find an answer:

Why does God allow disasters to happen?
Why does God allow people to die of starvation?
Why did uncle Jim lose his sight?
Why are there so many wars?
Why are there so many diseases for which we cannot find a cure?

It is not entirely satisfactory to say that these problems arise because of human folly and stupidity because so often innocent people seem to suffer. Christian people believe that one day solutions will be found to these mysteries. God's word teaches that at present we only see things vaguely as through a dark glass but that one day, if we have faith, we will be privileged to see clearly and understand the great mysteries of life.

Reading	1 Corinthians 13, 11–13 (or read the whole chapter)
Prayers	No 51 and No 56
Hymn	'Immortal, invisible God only wise' 'Father I place into your hands the things that I can't do'

Hallowe'en *Week 8*

Aim	To show the real significance of Hallowe'en
Visual Aid	An apple suspended on a string

Today we are going to think of the real meaning of Hallowe'en. 'Hallow' is an old word meaning 'saint' and Hallowe'en is short for All Hallows Eve, that is the evening before All Saints Day which falls on 1st November.

In pre-Christian times people celebrated the end of summer with a festival to thank the gods for the crops that had been gathered in for the winter. Superstition was rife. People thought that spirits returned to their homes at this time of year. Farmers lit fires in their fields and then carried the burnt wood to the four corners of their land to ensure healthy crops and livestock the next year.

The important day for Christians should be All Saints Day. Alas, in the early days of the church and through into the Middle Ages, a good deal of pagan superstition remained. Apples were thought to be a magical fruit. Girls would eat an apple and comb their hair at the stroke of midnight. They looked into a mirror to see the reflection of the person they were supposed to marry. If a long unbroken strip of apple peel was thrown over the left shoulder it would take the shape of the initial of their future husband's name.

In Scotland a game was played with three bowls, one filled with clear water, another with muddy water while a third remained empty. Boys were then blindfolded and invited to put their hand into one of the bowls. If the boy chose the clear water he would marry a fair maiden. Choosing the muddy water meant he would marry a widow. But if he chose the empty bowl this was an indication that he would never marry.

Two chestnuts were roasted. If one cracked and jumped it was a sign that a sweetheart would be untrue. If both chestnuts blazed, the two lovers would marry.

Even today at Hallowe'en parties, traditional games are played, like ducking apples and bobbing apples. (*Demonstrate the latter* – with hands tied behind their backs, pupils try to bite apples suspended by a string above their heads.)

Ducking apples is a similar game with apples floating in a bowl of water. We shan't try that game in our assembly – for obvious reasons!

Enjoy your Hallowe'en parties but don't get carried away by superstitions.

Christian application

Instead of thinking of ghosts and spirits, luck and superstitions, how much better it would be to think of all the good people who have followed Jesus' example and who we think of as saints. Here now is quite an amazing fact: you too can be saint, for the New Testament teaches that anyone who trusts in the Lord Jesus Christ and follows him is a saint.

Reading	Ephesians 1, 1–6 Paul always addresses the believers as saints.
Prayer	No 33 or No 15
Hymn	'For all the saints' 'How sweet the name of Jesus sounds'

Note References from *The Party Handbook* by Malcolm Bird and Alan Dart (Pavilion Books)

Clangers

Week 9

Aim To learn to say what we mean

Have you ever been amused by blunders made by sports commentators? Here are some examples of statements which some commentators are reported to have made:

DAVID COLEMAN: 'And they come through absolutely together with Wells in first place.'

ALAN WEEKS: 'This is the 17-year-old who has really plummeted to the top.'

TONY GUBBA: 'He can't afford to be beaten because if he is, he'll be beaten.'

TED LOWE: 'One mistake here could win or lose the match either way.'

RON PICKERING: 'He is going up and down like a metronome.'

DAVID VINE: 'I am speaking from a deserted and virtually empty Crucible Theatre.'

EDDIE WARING: 'Let's see where that move started. And it started from its origins.'

PETER JONES: 'Lawrenson slipped the ball through to Williams and he beat Shilton from 35 yards and you don't beat Shilton from 35 yards.'

DAN MASKELL: 'Oh! That cross-court angle was so acute it doesn't exist.'

DAVID COLEMAN: 'This is a truly international field, no Britons involved.'

RICHIE BENAUD: 'His throw went absolutely nowhere near where it was going.'

FRED TRUEMAN: 'That was a tremendous six: the ball was still in the air as it went over the boundary.'

RICHIE BENAUD: 'The slow-motion re-play doesn't show how fast the ball was travelling.'
JOHN LOWE: 'He's ranked number three in Britain, number four in the world. You can't get any higher!'

I wonder how many of these celebrities wish they could have had a chance to re-phrase their statements? But they have given us a lot of fun!

How often we wish we could have our time over again. We wish we had not said what we did say. Perhaps we said something which conveyed the wrong impression or maybe we were not as truthful as we should have been. Sometimes we say hurtful, harmful things which greatly upset our friends and we wish we could 'unsay' those words, but the damage has been done.

Always try to think before you speak.

Christian application
The Bible warns us of the danger of careless talk, of the great harm our tongues can do if we do not learn to control them.

Reading	James 3, 3–8
Prayer	No 35
Hymn	'May the mind of Christ my Saviour'
	'Heavenly Father may thy blessing'

Thank you! *Week 10*

Theme	Showing appreciation makes for good relationships
Visual Aid	Cards with the words **Keep Off** and **Please Keep Off, Thank You**

Susan was only five but it was a big day for her, she was going to her first party. Her mother took her along to her friend's house but before leaving she whispered to Susan 'Don't forget to say thank you'.

Now she was only a child, but it is a fact that many adults forget to say 'Thank you'. Have you ever held a door open for an adult? I hope they had the good manners to say 'Thank you'. When you are going into a shop and you hold the door open for the person who is following and they just walk straight through without making any comment you may wish you hadn't bothered!

What do you think of a notice like this?

KEEP OFF

It is a very threatening, rude notice. Wouldn't you have preferred it to say –

PLEASE

KEEP OFF

THANK YOU!

After all, it doesn't cost anything to be polite and courteous and it does go a long way towards making a happier place. We all like to feel that our efforts have been appreciated.

Christian application
Jesus must have felt the same. Our reading today tells how he healed ten lepers and was saddened that only one returned to say 'Thank you!'.

Reading Luke 17, 11–19
We have so much for which we should say 'Thank you' to God. Let us not forget to do so.

Optional conclusion This is the time of year when we thank God for bringing peace to our land. It was on the eleventh hour of the eleventh day of the eleventh month in 1918 that the armistice was signed to bring to an end the First World War. People at the time thought it would be the war to end all wars. Sadly the nations had not learned the lesson of that terrible conflict. Only twenty-one years later the world was plunged into a second great war. Since then there has been savage warfare in many parts of the world. But today we remember in our prayers men and women who fought that we might have freedom from tyranny and we thank our Heavenly Father for that freedom and peace.

Prayer No 5
Hymn 'Thank you for every new good morning'
'Thank you Lord for this fine day'
'Now thank we all our God'

The Lord's Prayer *Week 11*

Aim To make the Lord's Prayer more meaningful

Hughie was only three but he had a remarkable vocabulary. He could say:

'Humpty Dumpty sat on a wall.'
'Happy Christmas.'
'Who is mummy's treasure then?'
'Hughie go to bed, good night.'
And lots more.

But he sometimes got mixed up and said things like: 'Humpty Christmas' and 'Happy Dumpty'!

This wasn't surprising, though, because Hughie was a budgerigar. Being a member of the parrot family he didn't really understand what he said. He spoke parrot fashion.

Do we sometimes fall into the trap of reciting things 'parrot fashion', without thinking of what we are saying? For example, have we ever stopped to think of the significance of the words of the Lord's Prayer which we use every day?

This might help you.

Our Father God is a loving Father to all his children, throughout the world, whatever their race or colour, to all who acknowledge him.

Who art in heaven Heaven is not just some vague, distant place up in the clouds. Heaven is around us and can even be within.

Hallowed be thy name This means that we praise, we worship and honour God who is holy.

Thy kingdom come We should all pray that God's kingdom of love will spread throughout the world.

Thy will be done on earth as it is in heaven Year by year we see what disasters happen when people seek to have their own way. How much better if we would ask God to let his will be done.

Give us this day our daily bread God does promise to supply all our needs. We should not ask him for luxuries but simply for the necessities of life.

And forgive us our trespasses That is, sins or shortcomings, for we have all fallen short of the standards God has set.

As we forgive those who trespass against us We can only ask God to forgive us if we are prepared to forgive those who may have wronged or offended us.

And lead us not into temptation There will always be temptations to overcome. In the Lord's Prayer we ask God to give us the strength to conquer temptation.

But deliver us from evil If we trust in God there is nothing to fear for we are in his hands.

For thine is the kingdom The heavens and the earth may pass away but God's kingdom lasts for ever.

The power and the glory God is almighty. He is a most wonderful Father.

For ever and ever With God there is no time. He is eternal.

Amen When we say this we mean 'so be it' or I agree with everything which has been said and want to make the prayer my own.

Here is some advice Jesus gave to his disciples about praying.

Reading Matthew 6, 5–8
Jesus went on to teach them the Lord's Prayer. As we say it together today let us try to mean the words and not just repeat it parrot fashion.

The Lord's Prayer

Hymn 'Abba Father let me be'

Barriers

Week 12

Aim To show that there are human barriers which should be broken down

Our topic today is barriers. You may well ask which barriers? There are many different types but they all have something in common. Barriers always prevent something from happening.

Many of you will have visited the (name of local stadium) football ground. There you will have seen barriers erected on the terracing to stop the crowd from surging forward when the local team is about to score a goal. If there were no barriers people could be knocked over and trodden underfoot.

You will all have seen the steel barriers constructed along the central reservation of motorways and some trunk roads. Though they do not prevent accidents they do help to make them less serious. Cars which go out of control are prevented from crossing the central reservation and so crashing head-on into oncoming traffic.

A barrier was constructed on the River Thames below London to prevent the city being flooded.

Barriers on other rivers are being considered for different reasons. It is thought that barriers across the Mersey and across Morecambe Bay could help to provide a source of water and hydro-electric power as well as creating leisuretime amenities.

Though barriers often serve a useful purpose there are those which create problems:

The language barrier creates a problem for people, particularly children, who have to live in foreign countries. These people have to work extra hard to overcome this obstacle.

Sadly there are racial barriers too, which spoil the harmony of a community. When people of different races, religions and cultures have to live together in the same country it is most important that racial barriers are removed. People must learn to respect each other's cultures and religions and so live harmoniously together.

Christian application

God's word tells us of another barrier which prevents something from happening. Our waywardness and rebellion, which the Bible calls sin, prevents us from having the happy fellowship with God which he had planned (see Isaiah 59, 2). God loves us so much that he has provided a way for this, the greatest of all barriers, to be removed (see John 1, 29).

Reading	John 1, 29–34 (Other useful references: Romans 3, 23; Romans 6, 23; 1 John 1, 8; John 3, 19; 1 John 1, 7; Romans 8, 1, 35 and 39; 1 Peter 3, 18.)
Prayer	No 46
Hymn	'Happiness is to know the Saviour'

Santa's mistake *Week 13*

Aim To emphasise the true significance of Christmas
Visual Aid A Christmas stocking

Today I have brought along my Christmas stocking, which I hope Father Christmas will fill in the early hours of Christmas morning while I am asleep! What a jolly fellow he is. He must work very hard making all those presents and visiting all those homes. And why does he not make himself ill eating all those mince pies and drinking all those glasses of sherry which are left out for him?

Here is a story for you. Bonfire night had only just been and gone when Father Christmas arrived at the local store for the weeks leading up to Christmas. Young Tim visited the store with his mother. Upon being introduced to Father Christmas the young lad promptly kicked him on the shin. I don't know what thoughts came into Santa's mind but he did manage to smile sweetly and pat Tim on the head, perhaps a little harder than he might have done! The young boy informed Santa that when he had visited the store to see him the previous year he had asked for a bicycle but when the great day arrived Tim had received a scooter instead. Santa had got it all wrong. He was then given a kick on the other shin.

The young lad had been let down by someone he had believed in and trusted. Of course, when Tim got a little older he realised that there was much he had to learn about the story of Father Christmas.

I wanted you to understand that there is no fantasy in the story of the birth of Jesus Christ. There are historical documents to prove that he was born two thousand years ago. Christmas is the birthday of Jesus Christ. It is a time when we should praise God that he loved the world so much that he sent his Son to be our Saviour.

Reading Matthew 1, 18–21
Prayer No 26
Carol 'Unto us is born a Son'

Merry Christmas *Week 14*

Aim To give an insight into Christmas customs in other European countries
Visual Aids Various cards with greetings in foreign languages (A group of pupils could be prepared in advance to help with this assembly.)

In just a few days you will be greeting your friends and relatives with the words **MERRY CHRISTMAS**. These cards show us the words which will be used by people in other European countries:

GLEDELIG JUL (Norway)
FRÖHLICHE WEIHNACHTEN (Germany)
JOYEUX NOËL (France)
BUON NATALE (Italy)
FELICES PASCUAS (Spain)

They all mean Merry Christmas. We are now to hear of some of the customs which will make Christmas a happy or merry time in other lands.

1ST PUPIL: At Christmas time in Norway children remember a little gnome called *Nisse*. Of course there is no such person, but the children pretend that he plays tricks on those who forget to put out a bowl of special porridge for him. He is supposed to guard all the farm animals. Late in the afternoon Norwegian children go round from house to house asking for sweets.

2ND PUPIL: German children like to leave letters on their window sills for *Christkind*, a winged figure, dressed in white robes and wearing a golden crown, who leaves gifts for them. Sometimes the letters are decorated with glue sprinkled with sugar to make them sparkle.

3RD PUPIL: In France the children leave their shoes by the fireplace to be filled with gifts by *Père Noël*. When Christmas morning arrives they also find sweets, fruit, nuts and small toys hanging on the Christmas tree. In cathedrals throughout France the story of Christ's birth is acted by children and by puppets.

4TH PUPIL: Celebrations start eight days before Christmas in Italy. Throughout Christmas Eve people have nothing to eat but when Christmas Day arrives the feasting begins. By twilight candles are lit round the family crib. Prayers are said and children recite poems.

5TH PUPIL: During the week prior to Christmas, Spanish families gather round their own Christmas mangers to sing, whilst children play tambourines and everyone dances. Shoes are placed on balconies on the night of 6th January in the hope that the Wise Men will fill them with gifts. Often bundles of straw are left for the camels.

As in our own Christmas customs there is so much which is make-believe. We must remember that there would be no Christmas if

Jesus Christ had not been born. Since Christmas is the birthday of Jesus we ought to give him a special gift. The carol tells us what that present should be:

> What can I give him
> Poor as I am?
> If I were a shepherd
> I would bring a lamb;
> If I were a wise man,
> I would do my part;
> Yet what I can I give him –
> Give my heart.

In this way our Christmas will be truly happy.

Reading Matthew 2, 1–11
Prayer No 27
Carol 'In the bleak mid-winter'

Carol service (taken by the pupils) *Week 15*

1ST PUPIL: The theme of our carol service is *Love*. Love from God and our love for God. Each of the carols we will sing mentions love. The first carol is 'Once in Royal David's city'.

2ND PUPIL: First Reading: Matthew 1, 18–23. The angel appears to Joseph.

3RD PUPIL: Our next carol warns us that if we do not listen carefully we may not hear the love-song brought to us by the angels. Let us sing the carol 'It came upon the midnight clear'.

4TH PUPIL: Second Reading: Luke 2, 1–14. The birth of Jesus.

5TH PUPIL: As we sing our next popular children's carol, we are reminded not only of God's love for us but that we should love him too. The carol is 'Away in a manger'.

6TH PUPIL: Third Reading: Matthew 2, 1–11. The wise men come to worship.

7TH PUPIL: The Christmas message is all about love. The writer of our next carol suggests that even in the face of the baby Jesus the observers could see love. 'Still the night, holy the night'.

8TH PUPIL: Fourth Reading: 1 John 4, 7–11. God's love for us in the gift of his Son.

9TH PUPIL: Our final carol echoes the mystery of God's amazing love: 'Christians awake'.

10TH PUPIL: Prayer: 'For God so loved the world that he gave his only begotten Son that whoever believes in him might have life.' Loving Father, we praise you and thank you this Christmas time for your love towards us and that you have shown your love in the gift of your Son Jesus who came to be our Saviour. Help us to show our gratitude and our love for you as we behave in a loving, caring, thoughtful way to other people. May the love which came down at Christmas be spread abroad throughout the world. Amen.

11TH PUPIL: The Grace: The grace of the Lord Jesus Christ, the love of God and the fellowship of the Holy Spirit be with us all, and those whom we love, this Christmas time and for evermore. Amen.

Year 1
Spring term

Records

Aim To encourage an ambitious approach to life as we begin a new year

Visual Aid A copy of *The Guinness Book of Records* (Five pupils could help with the assembly.)

It is a new year tradition that we should ponder over the achievements of the past and decide what should be our ambitions for the year which lies ahead. Many past achievements have stood as records for years and are listed in *The Guinness Book of Records*. Here are a few for you to consider.
(*Note*: the following statistics will need up-dating from time to time.)

1ST PUPIL: The longest single unbroken apple peeling on record is 52.51 metres, by Kathy Wafler of the USA on 16th October 1976.
2ND PUPIL: The longest time ever recorded for balancing on one foot was 34 hours, achieved by Lelslie Silva in Sri Lanka on 6–8 April 1991.
3RD PUPIL: An American, David Stein, created the longest bubble on 6 June 1988. It was 15.2 metres long. He used a simple bubble wand and ordinary washing-up liquid and water.
4TH PUPIL: The greatest height from which fresh eggs have been dropped without breaking is 198 metres. The eggs were dropped from a helicopter in 1979 on a golf course in Japan.
5TH PUPIL: If you had the distasteful job of licking the stamps for your Christmas cards then how about this for a record? John Kenmuir of Brisbane, Australia, licked and affixed 393 stamps in 4 minutes on 26 September 1990.

As we look to the new year we could well set ourselves more worthwhile tasks or records to achieve. Here are some suggestions:

1 Try to make this a record year for attendance.
2 Try to make it a record year for good behaviour.
3 Try to ensure that we make record progress with our studies.
4 Try to make this a record year for contributions to charity, etc.

Christian application
The Bible tells us of a most amazing record. Our reading tells of the greatest love one person can show for another.

Reading John 15, 9–14

Jesus has shown his love for us by coming into the world and laying down his life for our sakes. Let us try to carry out the Lord's wish in this new year by having a real love and concern for others.

Prayer No 42
Hymn 'Let there be love shared among us'

Mars

Week 2

Aim To encourage a good balance between work and play
Visual Aid A Mars bar

Put up your hands if you can tell me what it is that helps you to work, rest and play.
Answer: *A Mars a day helps you work rest and play*. This is the slogan of the manufacturers of the famous chocolate bar.

It is also good advice for healthy and successful careers at school, for a proverb states, 'All work and no play make Jack a dull boy'. On the other hand we should not expect to succeed if we neglect our work. There must be a sensible balance of work and play. We need energy to play but we also need to be rid of surplus energy if we are to settle down effectively to our studies. Rest, too, is essential. 'Early to bed, early to rise, makes a man healthy, wealthy and wise.'

Christian application
God's word teaches us that if we do not work we should not expect to eat (2 Thessalonians 3, 10). Those who are capable of working should not shirk it.

Jesus promises to give us the rest we require. 'Come to me and I will give you rest', meaning relief from the heavy burden of worry we may have (Matthew 11, 28).

Reading Romans 12, 1–8
Prayer No 32
Hymn 'Make me a channel of your peace'

Influenza

Week 3

Aim To show that how we live influences others

Mary arrived home from school with a headache. This got worse as the evening progressed. She then started sneezing. During the night she developed a nasty cough, streaming eyes and a sore throat. One minute she was shaking and shivering, the next she went into a hot sweat. After a long restless night she did try to get up for school but her legs wouldn't support her and she was so dizzy that the room seemed to be going round.

Mary's mother phoned the doctor and described the symptoms. 'Get her to stay in bed for forty-eight hours. Keep her warm. Give her plenty to drink. She's got 'flu! There is an epidemic going round,' said the doctor.

The word 'flu is short for influenza, a sort of severe, feverish cold which is catching, that is, the illness can be passed from one person to another.

Fortunately it doesn't usually last more than a couple of days and, having taken the doctor's advice, Mary was soon feeling much better.

In another sense we all have influenza, for the name of the illness comes from the Latin word *influentia* from which we also get the word 'influence'. 'Influence' is something which is catching. By the way we behave and speak to others, we influence their behaviour. Are we an influence for good or bad? How often we hear someone say, 'It wasn't really my fault, So-and-so told me to do it and said it would be all right. I was influenced by her.'

The message for us is that we should take care not to be led astray by the bad influence of others and should be determined to be a good influence ourselves.

Christian application
God will one day require each of us to show whether we have made the best use of our time and talents. It will be no good saying 'I was led astray by others'.

Reading	Romans 14, 10–13
Prayer	No 37
Hymn	'Follow, follow, I would follow Jesus'

Neighbours

Week 4

Aim	To encourage neighbourliness
Audio Aid	Recording of the theme tune to the soap opera, *Neighbours*

The music we have just heard introduces the theme of today's assembly: that is, being good neighbours. Many popular television programmes and soap operas exploit the theme of neighbourliness, often revealing how much petty squabbling and gossip goes on. The following stories happen to be true!

Story 1: Tom was looking forward to Christmas, but before he could begin to relax he had some last-minute parcels to deliver on Christmas Eve, for he was the local postman. He drove to an outlying district of the town in his mail van and pulled up outside the door of a terraced house. The parcel he had to deliver was obviously a wigwam from a mail order firm. As he rang the door bell, Tom felt pleased that he was arriving just in time with a child's Christmas present. He waited a while but there was no reply at number 17. The obvious solution occurred to him and he speedily went next door to number 19.

'Would you mind taking in this parcel for your neighbour at number 17?' said Tom. 'Oh no, love,' came the immediate reply, 'I couldn't do that, we are not on speaking terms!'

Fortunately the people at number 15 were in a more neighbourly frame of mind.

Story 2: The presenter of a radio phone-in chat show had invited comments from listeners on the subject of whether people nowadays were less neighbourly. A gentleman phoned to tell of his experience.

'My wife and I have recently moved house, having lived for four years at our previous address. On the morning our furniture was being loaded into the removal van, our next-door neighbour came round to speak to my wife. She explained why for the past four years she had never spoken to either of us. It was because she had had an argument with the people who lived in our house before we came.'

What a fine state of affairs! When a person quarrels with another, invariably both parties suffer. Unnecessary problems always arise when people are not on speaking terms. If only individuals would discuss their differences and resolve them in a neighbourly way!

Christian application

The teaching of Jesus on this subject is very clear. Listen to the story which Jesus told in order to show the lawyer who his neighbour was.

Reading Luke 10, 25–37

You would have expected the priest and the Levite to have helped the man who had been attacked and robbed, but it was the most unlikely person who came to his aid, a Samaritan, an enemy.

Who is *my* neighbour? Not just the person who lives next door!

	We are expected to treat everyone with respect – even people we don't like.
Prayer	No 1
Hymn	'When I needed a neighbour' 'Forth in thy name I go'

Crying wolf

Week 5

Theme Truthfulness

Story 1: Susan's mother called up to her. 'Come on down, Susan your breakfast is ready and you are going to be late for school.'

Back came the reply 'I don't want any breakfast, I've got a bit of a headache and I don't think I'm fit to go to school!' Now Susan's mother knew full well that this was a regular ploy when Susan was due to hand in homework and hadn't done it, or when a lesson was time-tabled which she didn't like. So she again said, 'Come on down Susan, it's no good trying that on, stop crying wolf!'

Story 2: The games teacher said to the boys of year seven (first year), 'I'll give you three minutes to get changed into your football kit, we are going to have a seven-a-side competition this morning.'

'Please sir!' said Nigel, 'I won't be able to take part because I have sprained my ankle.' 'Well now,' said the teacher, knowing well that Nigel was one of the few boys who didn't enjoy games, 'show me your excuse note from your parents. You haven't got one, eh? Don't tell me you are trying to get out of games again, crying wolf I call it.'

Though you may know what it means to 'cry wolf', it is possible you don't know how the saying originated. It comes from a very old fable by Aesop. I'll read it to you.

The shepherd boy and the wolf
A shepherd boy who tended his flock on a hillside not far from a village, often amused himself by crying, 'Wolf! Wolf!' so that he might laugh at the villagers who came running to his assistance. The trick had succeeded several times until one day the boy did see a wolf about to savage his sheep.

This time he cried 'Wolf! Wolf!' in earnest.

It was when no one came to his assistance that he learned, too late, that liars are not believed even when they tell the truth. The villagers, supposing him to be at his tricks again, paid no attention to his cries and the wolf carried off one of the sheep.

The moral is that people who tell lies are not believed even when they speak the truth.

Christian application

Reading Ephesians 6, 10–18

Truth is an important part of the armour we must wear if we are to be protected from all that is evil. 'Wear the belt of truth.'

Prayer No 35

Hymn 'Soldiers of Christ arise'
'Make me a channel of your peace'

Barometers

Week 6

Aim Helping to cope with life's storms

Visual Aid A barometer (aneroid)

Do you recognise this? What is it used for?

Let me explain how it works. A barometer is a measure of atmospheric pressure and can be read in units which are called millibars. In a mercury barometer a column of mercury is balanced in a glass tube by the pressure of the atmosphere. The glass tube is closed at one end and curved up at the other end, which is open. The air presses on the mercury at the open end, forcing it up the tube. The movement of the mercury shows changes in atmospheric pressure.

This type is more common (*show the aneroid barometer*), it is called an aneroid barometer. Instead of having a column of mercury it has a shallow metal cylinder. The distance between the faces can be changed by the air pressure as the air is partly removed from the box.

One barometer measures the movement of the mercury; the other barometer – the aneroid – measures the distance apart of the faces of the metal cylinder. This measurement is transferred to a scale measured in millibars. To help us understand what effect changes in atmospheric pressure are likely to have on the weather, the scale also shows a description of what the weather should be like. If the needle points to 950 millibars, for example, the conditions could be *Stormy*. At the other end of the scale, 1050 millibars indicates *Very Dry* weather. The full scale reads *Stormy*, *Rain*, *Change*, *Fair*, *Very Dry*.

You will have heard people say 'There are not two days alike'. Certainly in the course of a week, in this country, we experience many different types of weather. We never seem to be absolutely certain what it is going to be like, but a barometer can give us a good indication, for if the needle is rising this is a good indication that the weather is improving. If it is falling then we should expect a deterioration.

So too in life we never know what the next day will bring. There are bound to be times when everything seems set fair for us, when we are feeling good, when everything seems to be working out just as we want it to. We would be most fortunate if we didn't encounter a few storms. There are bound to be days when we feel a little off-colour or when we have the occasional set-back, but we may also have to contend with the real storms of life. It is a fact that we must face up to. Accidents do happen and we, ourselves, could be unfortunate victims. Later in life we may have to cope with a situation where we lose our job and are out of work. One of the most stormy periods of a person's life is when a relative, someone they love, dies. This is a fact of life which we will all have to face up to one day.

But fortunately we never know what the next day will bring. If we did know then we would worry all the more. As it is, we should hope for the best and live our lives fully and confidently, being determined to make our own contribution to the well-being of others.

Christian application
Now listen to some words from the Bible which tell us not to worry but to look to the future with confidence. Jesus said, 'Do not be anxious about your life, what you shall eat or what you shall drink, nor about your body, what you shall put on, . . . your heavenly Father knows that you need them all' (Matthew 6, 25 and 32). 'Let not your heart be troubled, believe in God, believe also in me . . . I go to prepare a place for you.' (John 14, 1 and 2). 'Lo I am with you always – to the end of the age.' (Matthew 28, 20).

Paul also wrote, 'We know in everything that God works for good with those who love him' (Romans 8, 28).

Reading	Matthew 6, 25–34, or John 14, 1–6
Prayer	No 56
Hymn	'The Lord's my shepherd' 'Will your anchor hold in the storms of life?' 'With Jesus in the boat' (for younger children)

Alarms

Week 7

Theme	Listening to our conscience
Visual Aid	An alarm clock

Today I want us to think about the importance of alarms. How many different types of alarm can you think of?

Hopefully the pupils will suggest the following:

1 *Fire alarm* (*Here will be an opportunity for the presenter to run through the school fire-drill.*)
2 *Smoke alarm* An essential item for any home. At the first sign of smoke it sets off a shrill siren. This gives warning to all in the house that a fire has broken out.
3 *Police car siren* Police cars often have to travel very quickly to the scene of an accident or crime. The siren warns other drivers to keep out of the way.
4 *Ambulance sirens* It is very important for ambulances to get patients to hospital in the shortest possible time. The siren warns other road users to make room for the ambulance.
5 *Burglar alarms* A necessary deterrent these days to those callous people who break into the homes of others. It is good to have a loud burglar alarm which alerts anyone in the house, frightens off the intruder and also warns neighbours.
6 *Air raid siren* All wars are caused in one way or another by human failure. One of the gravest tragedies of war is that innocent civilians and children inevitably suffer. Air raid sirens sound to warn of imminent danger so that people can take cover and protect themselves.
7 *Alarm clock* (*demonstrate*) If you do not have one of these then you certainly should have one. Maybe one or two pupils (who shall be nameless!) should buy themselves a good alarm clock so that they will be able to arrive at school on time. A repeater alarm may be the most sensible investment!

Finally I mention one more alarm, for we all have an inbuilt alarm system which warns us when we are doing something we should not do and reminds us when we are not being entirely truthful. It is our conscience; that inner voice which tells us how to behave.

Christian application

If ever our conscience tells us we have done wrong we should put matters right with the person we have hurt and also with God because he grieves, too, when his children behave badly.

If we say sorry to God, we know he will forgive us because he sent his son Jesus into the world to die that we might be forgiven.

Reading I John 1, 5–10
Prayer No 14 or No 25

Hymn 'There is a green hill far away'
'Lord Jesus Christ, you have come to us'

The old violin

Week 8

Aim To show that we all have an important part to play
Visual Aid A violin
Audio Aid To begin the assembly, an extract from, say, Mendelssohn's *Violin Concerto* or Bach's *Air on the G-String*

It was very dusty and scratched and badly out of tune but the auctioneer held it up and asked the people to make their bids. The contents of the old mansion house were being auctioned off following the death of the owner and, last of all, the auctioneer came to this old violin which had been found in an attic. Without optimism he invited the bids. 'I'll give you five pounds,' said one person. Then reluctantly a second said, 'I'll give you six!'

'Going for six pounds to the man in the brown coat, going once, going twice . . .'

Suddenly an elderly, grey-haired gentleman rushed from the back of the hall and had a word with the auctioneer. He then dusted the instrument, tuned up the strings and played a tune which was so moving that several of those present were near to tears. He then quietly resumed his place.

'Now how much will you bid?' said the auctioneer.

'I'll give you one thousand pounds,' 'I'll give you two,' 'I'll give you three . . .'

The auction was completed, but the topic of conversation as everyone left was what had changed the value of the old violin. All concluded that it must have been the touch of the master's hand. What at first had appeared to be a very ordinary violin, of not much use or worth, had been transformed into something which could bring pleasure and enjoyment beyond imagination.

Is it not so with our lives? We may feel that we are unimportant, that there is little we can do to help others, but given the right circumstances we can make a valuable contribution to the life of our school. Don't let your talents go unused.

Christian application
It was the master musician who tuned up the violin and changed its value; the touch of the master's hand. When Jesus influences our lives what a difference he makes, what an improvement! Several

times in the New Testament we read of Jesus touching someone and so transforming their lives. His touch gave the dumb their speech, the blind their sight, made the lame walk. He longs to use ordinary people and promises to give them his strength.

Reading Matthew 11, 1–6
Prayer No 8
Hymn 'Father I place into your hands'

Mothering Sunday

Week 9

Aim To encourage a grateful appreciation for the love of parents
Visual Aid A Mother's Day card; a poster with the word **Simnel**

Visit any card shop in towns throughout the country at this time of year and you will find children of all ages selecting and buying suitable cards to give to their mothers on Mother's Day.

But Mother's Day or Mothering Sunday: which is the correct name? In fact the two have different origins and just happen to be celebrated on the same day.

Mother's Day is simply a special day in the year when we show our love and appreciation for all the care and help given to us by our mothers. It is an American idea started in 1906 but copied by many other countries throughout the world, though not all on the same date. In Australia, for example, Mother's Day is celebrated round about the second Sunday in May.

Mothering Sunday is the day in mid-Lent when children traditionally visit their mothers. It is the day when many Christians remember Jesus' own mother Mary. In centuries gone by children used to leave home at a very early age, even as young as ten years of age. They would go to work as apprentices or maids and would hardly ever have time to visit home. But in the seventeenth century employers would give these young employees a day's holiday on Mothering Sunday so that they could visit their family. They would take gifts of flowers, or cakes called Simnel cakes.

There are different stories about how the cake came to be called **Simnel**, but this is the story I like best.

One day a brother and a sister who were going to visit their mother on Mothering Sunday decided to make her a cake. Simon said 'We'll make it a very special cake, baked in the oven,' but his sister, Nell, thought it would be better to boil the cake, which was a very common way of making a cake in those days. They couldn't agree which would be the best so in the end they compromised. Simon baked a cake and Nell boiled one and they stuck the two together. They had made the first Sim-Nell cake.

Whatever gift you take to your mother on her special day, I'm sure it will be appreciated. It's the thought that counts. Parents don't usually ask for any reward for looking after their children, but it is right and proper to let them know how much we think about them, for they have given us the greatest gift, life itself.

Christian application

Jesus himself set us an example in this respect, for we are told in Luke's gospel that when Jesus was twelve years of age he went down with his parents to Nazareth and was obedient to them. After all, he was carrying out his Heavenly Father's wishes, for he had been taught the commandments.

Reading	Exodus 20, 1–17. Honour your father and your mother.
Prayer	No 15 or No 16
Hymn	'For the beauty of the earth'

Spring

Week 10

Aim	To show the wonders of creation
Visual Aids	A picture of a spring scene; a display of daffodils
Audio Aid	To start the assembly, 'Spring' from Vivaldi's *The Four Seasons* (Two pupils may be asked to assist with the presentation of this assembly.)

At springtime, more than at any other time of the year, English people who have gone to live abroad get a yearning to return home to see spring flowers coming to life, blossom forming on the trees, hedgerows turning green once more.

Poets, musicians and artists have found spring to be a most thrilling subject. Here are two poems which capture the atmosphere.

1ST PUPIL: *Home Thoughts from Abroad* by Robert Browning.

Oh, to be in England
Now that April's there,
And whoever wakes in England
Sees, some morning, unaware,
That the lowest boughs and the brushwood sheaf
Round the elm-tree bole are in tiny leaf,
While the chaffinch sings on the orchard bough
In England – now!

And after April, when May follows,
And the whitethroat builds, and all the swallows!
Hark, where my blossomed pear-tree in the hedge
Leans to the field and scatters on the clover
Blossoms and dewdrops – at the bent spray's edge –
That's the wise thrush; he sings each song twice over,
Lest you should think he never could recapture
The first fine careless rapture!
And though the fields look rough with hoary dew,
All will be gay when noontide wakes anew
The buttercups, the little children's dower
– Far brighter than this gaudy melon-flower!

2ND PUPIL: *Daffodils* by William Wordsworth.

I wandered lonely as a cloud
That floats on high o'er vales and hills,
When all at once I saw a crowd,
A host of golden daffodils;
Beside the lake, beneath the trees,
Fluttering and dancing in the breeze.

Continuous as the stars that shine
And twinkle on the milky way,
They stretched in never-ending line
Along the margin of a bay:
Ten thousand saw I at a glance,
Tossing their heads in sprightly dance.

The waves beside them danced, but they
Outdid the sparkling waves in glee:–
A poet could not but be gay,
In such a jocund company:
I gazed – and gazed – but little thought
What wealth the show to me had brought:

For oft when on my couch I lie
In vacant or in pensive mood,
They flash upon that inward eye
Which is the bliss of solitude,
And then my heart with pleasure fills,
And dances with the daffodils.

In the animal world too there are new signs of life as those animals which have hibernated for the winter become active again.

Spring is a good time for us to approach our work and our play with renewed vigour.

Christian application
Our Bible reading tells us that God, who has created such a wonderful world, cares and provides for each one of us.

Reading	Matthew 6, 25–33
Prayer	No 52
Hymn	'For the beauty of the earth'
	'All things bright and beautiful'

Message in a bottle *Week 11*

Aim	To show the folly of keeping things bottled up
Visual Aid	An old bottle (coloured glass) with cork

Kevin and his younger sister Karen were indulging in their favourite pastime, fishing. The holiday resort where they were enjoying their summer holiday had a secluded, rocky beach which was ideal for them. They had been sitting on the rocks for some time but had not caught anything when suddenly Karen saw something bobbing up and down in the water. As it got nearer Kevin took his net in one hand and held on to Karen at the same time. 'Got it!' exclaimed Kevin. But what was it they had caught? As Kevin turned the net over on a sandy patch it was revealed that he had caught a glass bottle (rather like this one). Their initial disappointment turned to excitement when they realised the bottle had a cork in it and there was a message inside the bottle. Eagerly they unravelled the small sheet of paper which, judging by its condition, had been in the bottle for quite some time. The message read:

'I need help, urgently.'

Clearly it was too late to do anything about it now. Whoever had sent that message would now be no longer in need of help! The message had been bottled up far too long. The incident did provide a talking point for the rest of the holidays.

Do you keep things bottled up? Maybe you are finding a subject at school particularly difficult and you get more and more confused the more you worry about it. Don't keep it to yourself. Your teachers will help. Perhaps there is some problem outside school and you don't know to whom you may turn. It isn't necessary to carry this burden on your own; there are people who can advise you, your parents, for example, or your school tutors.

Christian application
Whatever our problem we should realise that our Heavenly Father cares and longs to help. Yet people often seem reluctant to pray to him. Instead they keep things bottled up. Listen then to this wonderful promise from God.

Reading Matthew 7, 7–12
Prayer No 10
Chorus 'Ask and it shall be given unto you'

Miracles

Week 12

Aim To show that Jesus can work wonders with what we give to him
Visual Aid A money box

The church roof was badly in need of repair. Immediate attention was needed if it was to be saved. But where could they possibly get the money they needed? At the week-end the vicar announced that he would hold a special gift day and asked his parishioners to give what they could.

Winston was only ten and didn't get very much pocket money, but he wanted to do what he could to help save the church. He opened his money box and counted out £1.23, which he was saving for his summer holidays. 'It's not very much' he said to the vicar, 'but it's all I've got, and you may have it if it is of any help.'

The vicar was so touched by the young lad's generosity that he mentioned it to the people who came along to the gift day. Many must have thought to themselves, 'If that young lad can give all he has then I must give generously'. The response was amazing, miraculous in fact! The target had been reached. The roof repairs could begin.

Now listen to a similar story from John's gospel. (Read John 6, 4–13, feeding the five thousand.)

Barley bread was the cheapest kind of bread and only eaten by the very poor. The fish were tiny, like sardines, and probably pickled. Although the boy had only a little, he was willing to give it to Jesus. As a result everyone was satisfied.

It often seems that we, like the boys in both our stories, have little to offer Jesus. We may be weak in health, shy, not very clever, but if we offer what we have to Jesus, he can do great things through us; he can still work miracles.

Prayer No 11
Hymn 'Father I place into your hands'

Hot cross buns

Week 13

Aim To show the importance of the cross
Visual Aid A hot cross bun

Most of you will, no doubt, be eating one of these on Good Friday. It is a hot cross bun. Years ago children would look forward to Good Friday because they would be able to have hot cross buns to eat. As they played in the street and skipped they would chant:

Hot cross buns, hot cross buns,
One a penny, two a penny,
Hot cross buns.
If you have no daughters
Give them to your sons,
One a penny, two a penny,
Hot cross buns.

(Three pupils could be rehearsed to demonstrate this.)

Like most things, they now cost far more than they used to in the old rhyme!

Why do the buns have a cross on the top? To remind us of the significance of the day when we eat them, Good Friday. It was on this day that Jesus was crucified upon the cross, such a humiliation and agony, for he had done no wrong. Because of the awful events of that day you would think it should have been called Bad Friday. But Christians know that without the events of that Friday there would be no Easter, no resurrection and no forgiveness, for, in the words of the hymn, Jesus 'died that we might be forgiven, he died to make us good'. It was indeed Good Friday.

Reading	Luke 23, 33–46 The crucifixion
Prayer	No 25
Hymn	'There is a green hill far away'
	'When I survey the wondrous cross'

Year 1
Summer term

Easter bunnies

Week 1

Aim	To illustrate the meaning of Easter
Visual Aid	A chocolate bunny and chocolate egg

Little children love to eat Easter eggs and chocolate bunnies. But why? The obvious answer is because they are extremely tasty. But what is the significance of eggs and bunnies, because all chocolate is tasty?

To find out the reason, we have to go back to the pagan goddess Eostre from whose name we get the word Easter. According to legend, the goddess kept an enormous bird as a pet which one day, in a fit of anger, she changed into a rabbit. Ever after, on the first day of spring, the rabbit remembered his days as a bird and built a nest, laying brightly coloured eggs in it. So now you know the origin of Easter eggs and Easter bunnies.

The Christian festival of Easter coincides with spring, a time when the world springs to life again after the cold, dreary winter. The egg, as it hatches into a baby chicken, typifies this new life. It is most appropriate at this time of year for Christians to remember that Jesus came to life again. He rose from the dead.

'He was crucified, died and was buried but the third day he rose again.' So we give thanks today not just for the new life which is seen in the world around us, but for the resurrection of the Lord Jesus Christ. 'Jesus Christ is declared to be the Son of God with power by the resurrection.'

Reading	Luke 24, 1–9
Prayer	No 28
Chorus	'He lives!'

Whose job?

Week 2

Aim	To demonstrate the need for teamwork

Here is a story about four people named Everybody, Somebody, Anybody and Nobody. There was an important job to be done and Everybody was sure that Somebody would do it. Anybody could have done it, but Nobody did it. Somebody got angry about that because it was Everybody's job. Everybody thought Anybody could do it, but Nobody realised that Everybody wouldn't do it. It ended up that Everybody blamed Somebody when Nobody did what Anybody could have done!

How often this situation occurs in schools, clubs, churches! How much better it would be if everybody played his or her part in, for example, keeping classrooms tidy, keeping the playground free of litter, and at home helping with washing the dishes and weeding the garden.

Christian application

1st Reading Matthew 25, 14–28. The parable of the talents

In this story a talent was a sum of money. Nowadays, however, we think of a talent as being a God-given gift or special ability. The man who received only one talent probably thought 'Why should I bother to use it? I will leave the task to somebody else!'

When asked to do a job it is very sad when our response is 'Why me? Why should I put the books away, I didn't get them out.'

Now here is another short story which Jesus told when he visited the temple.

2nd Reading Matthew 21, 28–31A

Can Jesus rely on us to do the tasks he had set?

Prayer No 37 or No 11

Hymn 'When I needed a neighbour'
(or, for very young children, 'O what can little hands do?')

Boomerangs *Week 3*

Aim To show that the way we behave affects other people

Visual Aid A boomerang, or a picture of one

You will all recognise this wooden object which is called a boomerang; and you will probably know that it is an ancient weapon developed by the original inhabitants of Australia, the Aborigines, to help them with their hunting.

The famous explorer Matthew Flinders described in his diary in 1802 having seen one of these inhabitants. His description of the weapon the Aborigine carried could have been of a boomerang. Here is an extract from his diary:

> 'Our attention was suddenly called by the screams of three women who took their children and ran off in great consterna-

tion. Soon afterwards a man made his appearance. He was of middle age, unarmed except with a wooden scimitar.'

The wonder of a boomerang is its precise aerodynamic form which enables it to fly accurately through the air and return to its thrower, unless en route it strikes some other object. In section a boomerang is similar to the shape of a modern aeroplane wing, which was developed thousands of years later.

Visitors to Australia are keen to buy boomerangs as a memento of their holiday. The authentic one usually has a leaflet explaining how to throw it correctly, that is to say: 'Throw at 45 degrees away from the wind direction with the flat side away from the wind and away from the body.'

Have you ever succeeded in getting a boomerang to return to you? Make sure you are supervised if you try.

The way we behave often acts like a boomerang. Here is an example of what can happen:

William had forgotten to do his maths homework and knew he would get into trouble. It wasn't the first time this had happened. There was still twenty minutes before the teacher was due to arrive for the first lesson, so William went into the classroom and waited his opportunity. It wasn't long before James, who always came top in maths, came in, put his homework book on the pile and went out again. Some of the others were horrified when they saw William sneak James' book from the pile and start to copy the homework but they didn't say anything. They were all afraid of William.

It was the following day when the maths teacher was giving out the books, having marked the homework, that he said: 'I want to congratulate William on an excellent homework, your solution to the problem was very well thought out and I'm very pleased that, for a change, you have handed in your homework on time. And now I would like you to come out to the front, William, and explain to the rest of the class how you worked out the solution!'

Of course the teacher knew very well what had been going on. As for William, his dishonesty had been like a boomerang – it had rebounded on him.

Christian application

The Bible tells us of another type of boomerang, which is called sin. 'Be sure your sins will find you out.' It is true that we all make mistakes and do or say things which we afterwards regret.

It is sensible, should this happen, to say that we are sorry to the person we have offended but also to our Heavenly Father, knowing that if we neglect to do so then our wrongdoing returns to us in the form of guilt. But God is a loving Father who always forgives his children when they say they are sorry.

Reading	1 John 1
Prayer	No 25
Hymn	'Heavenly Father may thy blessing' 'Father lead me day by day'

Independent Herbert *Week 4*

Aim To show that there are times when we are wise to accept the help and advice of others

Herbert had an important interview in London at 11am. He was sure everything would be all right, he would see to that. In fact he was so confident in his own ability to handle affairs that his associates called him 'Independent Herbert'.

He set out in plenty of time for his appointment, thinking he would create a good impression by turning up in his brand new car. But, a few minutes after leaving home, the car spluttered to a halt. Herbert wasn't worried, he was sure he could fix it; he got out and opened the bonnet. 'Are you having trouble?' said a neighbour, slowing down in his car, as he saw Herbert obviously having difficulty, 'Can I be of assistance?' 'Oh no!' said Herbert, 'I can fix it all right, I don't need your help.' But as he saw his neighbour's car disappear down the road, he realised that he had forgotten to put petrol in his car and he was miles away from a garage.

Herbert didn't panic, he took his briefcase, locked up his car and set out to walk to the railway station. 'Can I give you a lift, I'm going to the station?' said a passer-by. 'That's all right,' said Herbert, 'I'll manage perfectly well on my own, thank you; it's not far to walk.'

It took longer than he thought. His train was due to leave in two minutes so he bought his ticket, deciding that he didn't need to bother asking which platform the train departed from, he would find out himself, he didn't need anyone to help him. Unfortunately he took so long getting to the right platform that he arrived just in time to see the train leaving the station. The next train would only be forty-five minutes and it would get him there in time, so he still wasn't worried.

On arrival Herbert rushed from the London station. 'Excuse me sir, would you like a taxi?' said the cabbie. 'No, I'll manage on my own; I'll catch a bus' came the reply. After wandering around for quite some time, he discovered there were no buses travelling in the direction he wanted to go, so once more he set out on foot.

When Herbert eventually arrived at his destination it was nearly 1pm. 'I'm very sorry, sir, the interviews were completed over half-an-hour ago. There's nothing I can do about it,' said the receptionist.

Herbert learnt an important lesson that day. Though it is often good to be independent and tackle your own problems, it is also very prudent sometimes to accept the help and advice of others. You will find that there are many people on hand to help you with your problems, should you not be able to cope on your own. Never be afraid to ask for help from your parents or your teachers if you can't manage by yourself.

Christian application
This sound advice can also be found in the Bible, for Paul says that we should 'Bear one another's burdens and so fulfil the law of Christ' (Galatians 6, 2). In our reading Jesus promises to help with our problems.

Reading Matthew 11, 28–30
Prayer No 16 or No 18
Our hymn is about helping those who have special needs.
Hymn 'When I needed a neighbour were you there?'

Manufacturer's instructions *Week 5*

Aim To show that God made us and knows all about us
Visual Aids A collection of manufacturer's instruction booklets

Whenever we buy a piece of new equipment or machinery, we do well to read carefully the manufacturer's instructions before we attempt to use the item.

Can you guess to which items these instructions refer?

1 Do not use oil, solvents, petrol, paint thinners or insecticides on this unit.

Do not expose the unit to moisture or to temperatures higher than 60°C.

Keep away from strong magnetic fields, excessive dust and humidity.

Hold the AC power plug by the head when removing from the AC outlet, since pulling the lead can damage the internal wires.

Remove the mains plug from the wall socket before cleaning the heads, pinch rollers, etc.

Did the last instruction give it away? The item is a stereo radio cassette recorder.

Here is the next one:

2 Warning – this appliance must be earthed. Remove the packing materials from the inside of the door but do not remove the plastic sheet that covers the perforations in the door screen.

Do not remove the plastic disc on the turntable drive shaft.

When you place the revolving tray into the oven, ensure the plastic ring and the spindle are in position.

The manufacturer will not be held responsible for damage cause by faulty use.

This item is a microwave oven.

Now for number 3:

3 Modification could affect performance, safety or durability, and may even violate governmental regulations. In addition, damage caused by modification will not be covered under warranty.

During the 'break-in' period do not drive for a long time at any single speed either fast or slow.

Keep people and combustible materials away from the exhaust pipe while the engine is running.

Obviously these instructions were supplied with a new motor car.

And next:

4 Whenever an operation button is pressed, the activated function is immediately indicated on the easy-to-see display. It shows you at a glance, in what operation mode the VTR is functioning.

Need I go on? The reference is obviously to a video recorder.

Finally, to what do you think these manufacturer's or maker's instructions apply:

Reading	Exodus 20, 1–17 (The Ten Commandments) God said 'Let us make man in our image, after our likeness,' Genesis 1, 26 'It is he that hath make us and not we ourselves.' Since God made us in the first place we would do well to read and follow the manufacturer's instructions!
Prayer	No 17
Hymn	'Now thank we all our God'

DIY

Week 6

Aim	To encourage self-reliance
Visual Aid	Nails, a piece of wood, a 13-amp plug, a paint brush

Your grandparents will remember the time when, if you wanted some nails, you would have to get them from the shop which specialised in such things, the ironmonger. And if you needed a piece of wood to repair the skirting board you would have to purchase it from a timber merchant. A new plug for the electric kettle could only be obtained from an electrician's shop, whilst a tin of paint or a brush would be sold by the painter and decorator.

Nowadays all these varied items and countless more may be bought at the local DIY store. Of course you know that the initials stand for 'Do It Yourself'. Not only is it more economical to do the job yourself but you will derive a great sense of achievement and satisfaction from a job well done. 'You'll never know what you can do until you try.' 'If a job is worth doing it is worth doing properly.'

You will be surprised how much you can do yourself if you put your mind to it. Take advice from others by all means, but don't just rely on them to do the work for you. **Do it yourself**.

Christian application

One thing you cannot do yourself, however, is earn forgiveness. God's forgiveness is a gift to those who say they are sorry and put their trust in him. We will never be able to boast that we earned God's favour.

Reading	Ephesians 2, 4–10
Prayer	No 14
Hymn	'In the name of Jesus we have the victory'

Note: A comparison could be made with the theme for week 4, 'Independent Herbert'. We need to find the right balance.

Bob's kite

Week 7

Aim To show how God can influence and work through people
An assembly for Whitsuntide

Visual Aid A kite

Young Bob used to go to the park every Saturday morning with his mother to fly his kite. It was like this one.

On this particular Saturday his mother left him playing by himself as she had some shopping to do. No sooner had Bob's mother disappeared out of sight when along came a gang of older, bigger boys who started teasing Bob.

'Why does your mother have to bring you to the park?'
'Why can't you come on your own?'
'You must be a sissy!'

These were the sort of taunts they made.

'Well,' said Bob, 'It's rather difficult because I have to cross a busy main road and my mother doesn't like me coming on my own.' This didn't make things any better. 'So have we,' interrupted a very rude boy. 'Don't you know your Green Cross Code? If you look both ways you will be all right!'

'Ah!' said Bob, 'That's the trouble, I can't look both ways, you see I'm blind.'

You can imagine how small those big boys felt. This time, filled with admiration for Bob's courage they asked, 'Well, how do you manage to fly a kite if you can't see? And what pleasure do you get out of it if you can't see it flying high up in the sky? Why do you seem to enjoy it so much?'

Bob thought for a moment and then replied, 'Although I can't see it, I can feel its pull!'

Throughout the ages, people have said the same about God. Although they cannot see him, they can feel his pull. God does help people. God does guide people. God does give strength to people who need it and who ask for it. Ordinary people can experience God's pull in their lives.

Reading Luke 11, 1–13 or 9–13 or Ephesians 3, 14–21

Prayer	No 6 or No 33
Hymn	'Lord of all hopefulness'

Who dun it?

Week 8

Aim	To encourage a persevering and enquiring mind
Visual Aid	The game *Cluedo*

I wonder if you have ever played this game. It is very absorbing, a real brain teaser! The idea is that you have to try to solve a mystery. A murder has been committed and you have to find out who did it, in which room and what was the murder weapon.

Was it Miss Scarlet with the candlestick in the lounge?
Or was it Colonel Mustard with the revolver in the library?
Or was it Professor Plum with the dagger in the study? And so on.

Well, 'Who dun it?' Although not grammatical that expression describes the mystery stories we like to watch on television. Why not read a 'Who dun it'? There are lots of excellent crime and detective novels in the library, they will hold you in suspense and mystery to the end. I always like to try to solve the mystery myself before I get to the end of the book. I'm usually wrong but it does give a sense of satisfaction when I am able to say 'I knew that is what really happened' or 'I suspected him all along!'

Life itself presents many mysteries and it is right that we should have an enquiring mind, that we should persevere in trying to find a solution to some of life's problems.

What lies beyond the horizon? This mystery was solved centuries ago when explorers discovered that the earth was a sphere.

What is it like on the moon? In more recent years space exploration has begun to give us the answer.

How can we cure cancer? How can we protect the ozone layer? How can we feed the world's starving millions? Many problems still have to be solved and questions still have to be answered, but we must realise that we are always learning. There will never come a time in our lives when we should think that we know it all.

Christian application
Here now is a Bible passage which reminds us that there are many unsolved problems in life. 'Now we see through a glass darkly but one day we will know the answers just as God even now knows us.'

Reading	1 Corinthians 13
Prayer	No 24 or No 34
Hymn	'Stand up, clap hands, shout thank you Lord' 'God moves in a mysterious way'

Pass it on!

Week 9

Aim To show that we have a duty to pass on good news (Eight pupils will be required to help with the presentation of this assembly.)

Mary Smith loves John Jones, pass it on! (*Care should be taken not to use names of pupils currently in the school.*) Pupils often indulge in that sort of mischief. We are now going to carry out a little experiment with the help of eight volunteers.

(*At this point the presenter whispers a message in the ear of the first pupil so that no one else can hear . . . 'My auntie Mary lives on her own; she has a cat called "Whiskers" which has just had five black and white kittens.'*)

I have just given a secret message to . . . (Pupil No 1) and now I'm going to ask her/him to pass it on to . . . (Pupil No 2) without anyone else hearing. Next – Pupil No 2 passes it on to No 3 and so on, until the message reaches the last in the line.

I'm now going to ask the last pupil to say what message s/he has just received.

(*Now the presenter will have to be prepared to say* ***either*** *'The message I gave in the first place was (repeat message). Although similar to the one which reached the end of the line quite a few words have been missed out and the facts changed a little';* ***or*** *'That message was nothing like the one I gave at the beginning'.*)

When messages are conveyed by word of mouth, errors usually creep in, the message gets changed. When we pass on information to other people we should be sure of our facts. Inaccurate gossip can create ill feeling and cause quarrels. Avoid idle gossip.

Christian application

Mark's gospel was the first of the four gospels to be written, probably about twenty to thirty years after the death of Jesus.

Until then the gospel story was passed on in the early Christian church by word of mouth. Judging by our little experiment you would have expected lots of errors and discrepancies, yet the eventual writers of the four gospels have produced accounts which are remarkably accurate. Between them we get a clear picture of Christ's birth, teaching, crucifixion and resurrection.

Now it's up to us! We are commanded to pass on the good news to others but we today do have a big advantage, we have God's written word to help us. Pass it on!

Reading	Matthew 28, 16–20
Prayer	No 22
Hymn	'God has given us a book full of stories'
	'Go tell it on the mountain'

Parallel lines

Week 10

Aim	To show how important it is to follow a good example
Visual Aid	Card with the symbol for parallel

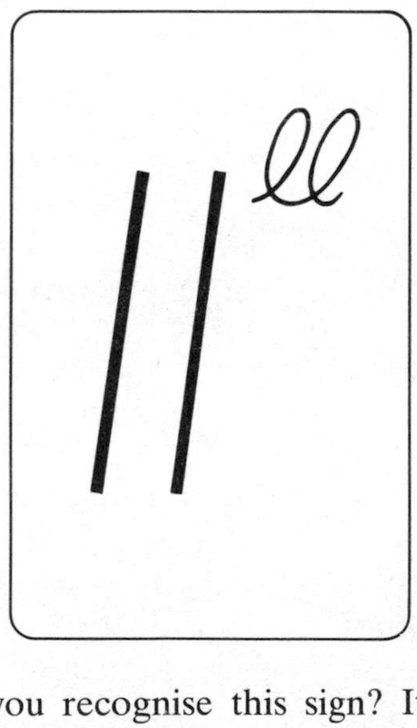

I wonder if any of you recognise this sign? It is the mathematical symbol for things which are parallel. Do you know what that means? When two lines are parallel they are exactly the same distance apart and no matter how long they are extended in either direction they would never meet.

Can you think of some parallel lines which stretch from Edinburgh to London? Correct! Railway lines. It's a good job railway lines are parallel. They could not be used if they were not.

Now see if you can spot any other things in this room which are parallel. (*Discuss.*)

Parallel things are constant, they don't wander away from each other – they stay alongside each other.

In a sense we should keep parallel. We can do so by following the good example of someone else and not allowing ourselves to be led astray.

Christian application

The best example to follow is that of Jesus for he will never lead us astray. He will always guide us and help us to stay on the straight and narrow path.

Reading	Hebrews 12, 1–3
Prayer	No 6
Hymn	'Follow, follow, I would follow Jesus'

Scales

Week 11

Aim	To show that even though we fall short of God's standards, he will forgive
Visual Aid	A set of kitchen scales A notice board with the words ***mene mene tekel parsin***

You will all have used a set of these, either at home or in lessons at school. When baking a cake it is most important to weigh the ingredients accurately.

Shopkeepers have to take great care that the commodities they sell in food shops are accurately weighed. There are people known as trading standards officers who check the scales from time to time to ensure that customers are not being cheated.

Now listen to this amazing story from the book of Daniel in the Old Testament.

Nebuchadnezzar's son Belshazzar was a lawless and godless pleasure-seeker. At a great banquet he even used the holy vessels from God's temple as wine goblets. Suddenly and mysteriously during the feast a hand appeared and wrote a message on the plaster wall in the royal palace:

Mene mene tekel parsin

Belshazzar's wise men could not interpret the mysterious writing on the wall. It was Daniel who was brought in to tell the king what it meant. Daniel explained:

Mene means that God has numbered the days of your reign and brought it to an end.
Tekel means that you have been 'weighed on the scales' and found wanting.
Parsin means that your kingdom is divided and given to the Medes and the Persians.

Belshazzar was a bad lot. He had been weighed in God's scale and in his sight Belshazzar had fallen short of the standards God had expected. He got what he deserved.

If we were to be weighed in God's scales we too would be found wanting for we have all, at times, done things of which we are ashamed and as Paul says, 'We all fall short of God's standards' (Romans 3, 23). The writing is on the wall for us!

Cheer up, though! There is good news, for if we turn humbly to God and say we are sorry he will forgive.

Reading	1 John 1, 5–9 (The story of Belshazzar's feast can be found in Daniel 5, and makes a good project.)
Prayer	No 19
Hymn	'Father lead me day by day'

Reports

Week 12

Aim	To encourage self-assessment of the year's work
Visual Aid	A blank report sheet/booklet

You will all be familiar with these (*show blank report*) and will have had discussions with your teachers about your own report for the year.

None of you will receive comments like the ones which a famous actor said, in an interview, he had received at school. His headmaster's report read as follows:

> 'Martin seems to think that he runs the school. If he continues in this manner one of us will have to leave.'
> 'Martin's hand-writing has improved sufficiently for us to see how bad his work really is.'

> 'Martin has set himself a low standard but has been unable to achieve it.'

Those reports were pretty scathing! What sort of report would you like to receive? The best reports I believe are those which say a pupil has done his or her best and has behaved well throughout the year. There is no reason why everyone should not be able to gain such a report.

Christian application
One day we shall each receive a different sort of report when the Lord assesses how faithful we have been. How marvellous it would be if he were to say to us:

> 'Well done, thou good and faithful servant.'

Reading Matthew 25, 14–30
Prayer No 49
Hymn 'Father I place into your hands'

Year 2
Autumn term

Bridges

Week 1

Aim 1 To assist the transition between year groups
2 To show that Jesus is like a bridge

Visual Aid A picture of a bridge, or if possible diagrams of different types of bridge: clapper, stone arch, cable suspension, cantilever, steel arch, floating, etc.

The building of bridges dates back to the times of primitive people. They were necessary if people were to be able to travel, even on foot, and negotiate rivers, chasms etc. The oldest surviving bridge in the world is the *slab stone bridge* over the River Meles in Smyrna, Turkey, and it dates from about 850 BC. But even in our own country we have bridges which date back to prehistoric times. Most famous of these are the *clapper bridges* of Dartmoor and Exmoor. They are simply slabs of stone placed across boulders. With the coming of the Romans, who became famous in the first century AD for their road building, we see the beginning also of *stone-built arched bridges*. Although they are now in ruins, remains can be seen in parts of Northumberland and Cumbria.

Nowdays bridges can be built to span far greater distances. The Clifton *suspension bridge* over the Avon Gorge near Bristol, was a remarkable feat of engineering, accomplished by the famous engineer Isombard Kingdom Brunel (1806 to 1859). The problem he overcame was how to span the deep gorge through which the river flowed. Another of his bridges is the famous Saltash bridge, spanning the River Tamar near Plymouth. Both bridges are still used today, illustrating the merit of Brunel's motto 'If a job is worth doing, it is worth doing properly'.

You may have heard people say, when confronted with a job which seems never ending 'It is like painting the Forth railway bridge'. That bridge in Scotland is so huge that by the time the painters have finished their task the first part is ready for painting again.

The world's longest bridge span is the main span of the Humber Estuary bridge: 1,410 metres long. The towers supporting this magnificent bridge are 162.5 metres tall and are 36mm out of parallel to allow for the curvature of the earth. The Japanese are likely to beat this record by the year 1998 with a bridge they are building.

San Francisco boasts two famous bridges, the Golden Gate bridge and the Oakland Bay bridge, both of which have withstood spectacular hurricanes and earthquakes. Perhaps the most well-known bridge of all is the Sydney Harbour bridge, nicknamed the

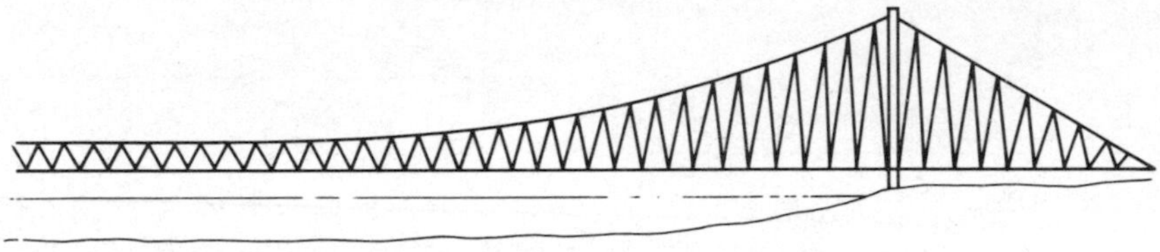

Golden Gate suspension bridge – San Francisco

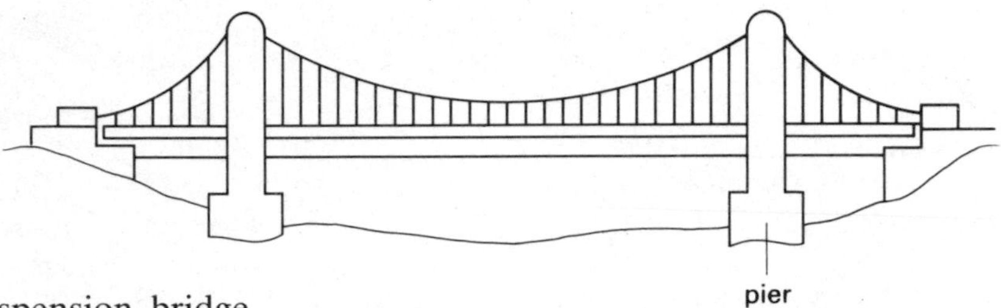

suspension bridge

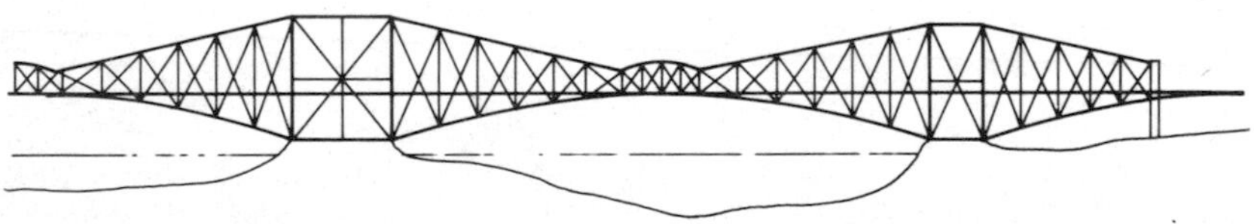

Forth railway bridge – cantilever and suspended span

'coat hanger', because of its shape, and the 'iron lung', because it kept so many people in work during the great depression between the two world wars.

A moving story is told of the bravery of a passenger on board the ferry *Herald of Free Enterprise* which tragically capsized just after setting out to cross the Channel from Zeebrugge. As the water was filling the boat this man formed himself into a human bridge so that other passengers could clamber to safety.

Bridges always enable people to cross over in safety from one side to the other. I suggest that you have all just crossed safely over a bridge, the imaginary bridge linking different school year groups. There will be many more bridges in life for you to cross. They help us to tackle with confidence the next experience of our lives. Now that you have crossed over to year . . . (*title of year group*) I hope you will soon settle in, making many new friends and making your own contribution to the life of the school.

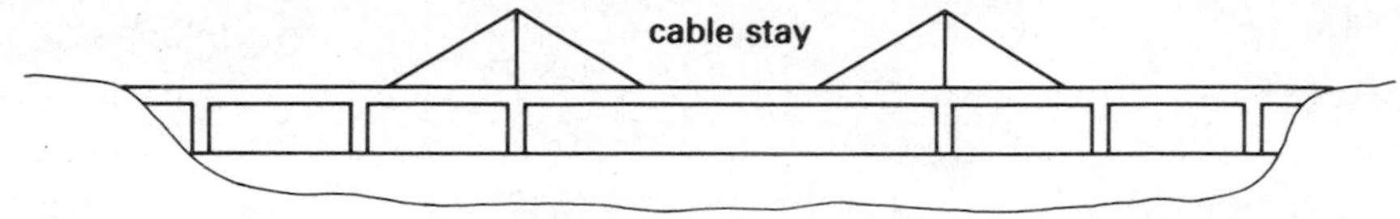

Erskine bridge – cable-stayed

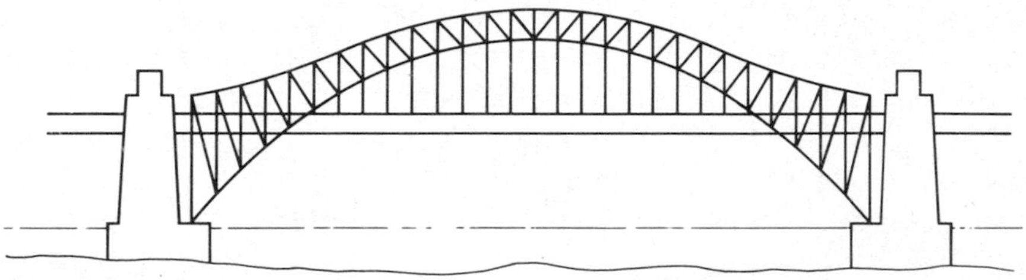

Sydney Harbour bridge – steel arch

Christian application
The Bible tells us of another great gulf which no mortal can span. It is the gulf between earth and heaven (see Luke 16, 26). Jesus has formed himself into a bridge so that we can come to God, through faith in him (see 1 Peter 3, 18).

Reading	John 14, 5–7
Prayer	No 45
Hymn	'One more step along the world I go'

Limelight
Week 2

Aim	To show that everyone has an important contribution to make to the life of the school

In the story I am about to tell you I will use six well-known expressions which have all been taken from the theatrical world. See if you can spot them.

The teacher announced to the class that she was going to *ring up the curtain* on a completely new topic. 'Please Miss,' said Timothy

Johnson, 'I already know a lot about that, my father is an expert.' Now Timothy's teacher didn't like being *up-staged* in this way and knew from past experience that Timothy liked to think himself an authority on just about everything, so she replied, 'I'm pleased to hear that, Timothy, but it will be *curtains for you* my lad if you don't co-operate. Your trouble is that you are always *playing to the gallery*, you always want to be *in the limelight*. I hope very much that you will try your best, learn all you can so that maybe one day you will have your *name in lights*.'

Well! How did you get on? Did you recognise the well-known sayings?

To ring up the curtain means to announce something new, as when the curtain is raised for the first time on a new play.

To be up-staged It would be very wrong in a stage production for someone who has a minor part to keep coming to the front of the stage so that the important characters are hidden. Actors don't like to be up-staged.

The limelight In the early days of theatre, before the advent of electricity, the front of the stage was lit by limelight. So the important actors often found themselves *in the limelight*.

Curtains It is always sad when a production finishes, and the particular moment is on the last night when the curtains close for the last time: that play will not be performed again. 'Curtains for you my lad' means that it is the end as far as the teacher was concerned, she wouldn't be giving any more privileges.

To play to the gallery Before microphones were invented, actors had to project their voices loudly so that the people sitting upstairs in the back row could hear. Timothy's problem was that he always tried to make himself noticed and the others in the class used to get fed up with him. It is often better to get on quickly with the task we have been given.

Name in lights The most popular and successful actors and actresses, those who played the most important roles, had their names printed prominently on the advertising posters and programmes. Then when electric neon signs were invented they had their names in lights.

As you begin a new school year and a new phase in your education you must realise that you can't all have your name in lights – you can't be in the limelight all the time – but everyone has a valued contribution to make to the life of our school and will receive recognition accordingly. Just as the success of a stage production doesn't depend on one or two talented artists but on the efforts of the whole cast, together with those who work behind the scenes, so the happiness and success of our school depends on each pupil playing his or her part.

Christian application
All that has been said applies even more to our service for the Lord Jesus Christ. There are those who are given special talents and called to play a prominent part. But the success of the Christian Church depends on ordinary people faithfully carrying out the tasks they have been given.

Reading Matthew 6, 1–4
Prayer No 9
Hymn 'Father I place into your hands'

Illusions

Week 3

Theme Jumping to the wrong conclusions
Visual Aids Three illustrations of optical illusions as shown

Today I want you to help me with a couple of experiments. Look carefully at the diagram (No 1 – see over).

How many of you think the two long lines are closer together at the left?

How many think they are closer together at the right? In fact, they are exactly the same distance apart all the way along. They are parallel. If they look further apart at the right this is an illusion.

Now let us study this diagram (No 2).

How many of you think the top line is longer?

How many think the bottom line is longer?

The answer is that although the bottom line seems longer, once again this is an illusion. They are both the same length.

Finally look at this third sheet. How many of you think it is a picture of a vase? It could also be two people facing each other, depending on whether you are looking for a white object on a black background or black objects on a white background.

We are often taken in by what we see and jump to the wrong conclusions. Here is a story to illustrate this point.

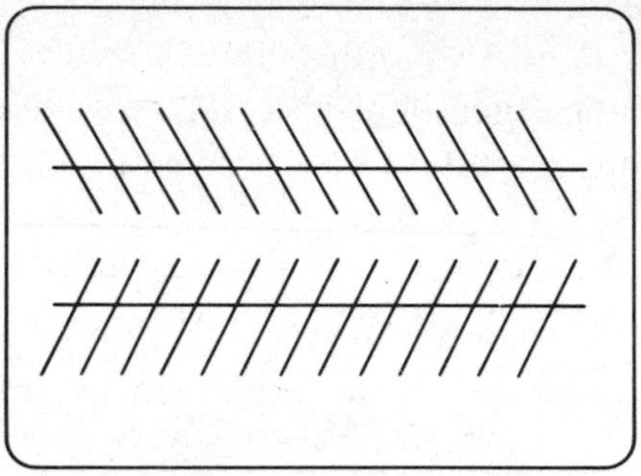

No 1

No 2

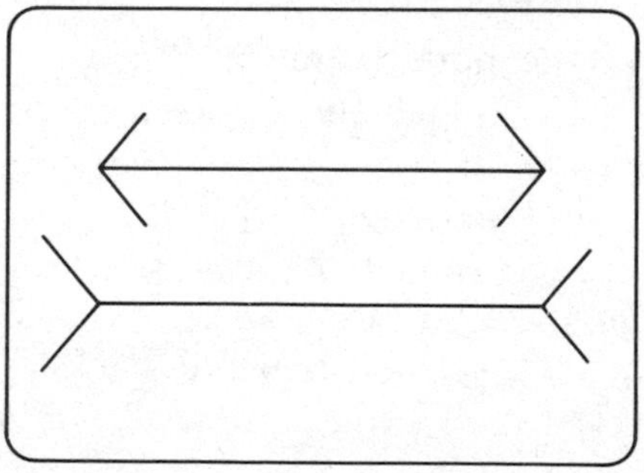

No 3

In North Wales there is a village named Beddgelert meaning 'Grave of Gelert'. Gelert was the name of a dog which belonged to Llewellyn the Great. Legend has it that Llewellyn returned home one day to discover that his infant son had been taken from his cradle. His faithful dog Gelert was there in the otherwise empty room and there was a pool of blood on the floor. Llewellyn concluded that the dog must have savaged his baby son and without further thought he killed the dog.

He then discovered that the dog had already been injured and when, moments later, he heard a baby's cry from the bedroom he rushed in to see his son placed safely on the bed.

Now he began to piece together the true facts. There had been an intruder in his home. His faithful dog Gelert, sensing danger, had carried the child to safety and had then turned on the intruder, getting injured in the process. The blood on the floor belonged to Gelert. In his remorse Llewellyn had a special grave made for his faithful dog. The village Beddgelert is named after him. The grave draws thousands of visitors each year.

The moral is: don't jump to the wrong conclusions.

Christian application

In this familiar story from the Old Testament, people jumped to the wrong conclusions. See if you can spot how many times this happened.

David had gone to visit his brothers, who were in the front line, ready to go into battle against the Philistines. (Read 1 Samuel 17, 23–43 and 48–51a using a modern translation.)

In the first place, David's brothers underestimated his ability. They thought he would have been better off at home, looking after sheep.

Next, King Saul was sceptical. But when David persuaded him to let him fight Goliath, Saul felt it necessary to let David have his own armour.

Finally, Goliath himself jumped to the wrong conclusion when he thought the young lad could not possibly harm him.

We may well have giants of a different sort to do battle against. Sometimes difficulties, problems or temptations loom so large in our lives that we feel we cannot cope.

The story we have just heard reminds us that we should not despair. We can tackle our own problems with God's help and with his guidance we can succeed.

Prayer No 23

Hymn ‘Who would true valour see’
‘Forth in thy name O Lord I go’

The church mouse *Week 4*

Aim To illustrate the need for commitment
Visual Aids Harvest produce

We begin our assembly today by listening to a poem.

Diary of a church mouse
by John Betjeman

Here among long discarded cassocks
Damp stools and half-split open hassocks,
Here where the Vicar never looks
I nibble through old service books.
Lean and alone I spend my days
Behind this Church of England baize.
I share my dark forgotten room
With two oil-lamps and half a broom.
The cleaner never bothers me,
So here I eat my frugal tea.
My bread is sawdust mixed with straw;
My jam is polish for the floor.

Christmas and Easter may be feasts
For congregations and for priests,
And so may Whitsun. All the same,
They do not fill my meagre frame.
For me the only feast at all
Is Autumn’s Harvest Festival,
When I can satisfy my want
With ears of corn around the font.
I climb the eagle’s brazen head
To burrow through a loaf of bread.
I scramble up the pulpit stair
And gnaw the marrows hanging there.

It is enjoyable to taste
These items ere they go to waste,
But how annoying when one finds

That other mice with pagan minds
Come into church my food to share
Who have no proper business there.
Two field mice who have no desire
To be baptized, invade the choir.
A large and most unfriendly rat
Comes in to see what we are at.
He says he thinks there is no God
And yet he comes . . . it's rather odd.
This year he stole a sheaf of wheat
(It screened our special preacher's seat),

And prosperous mice from fields away
Come in to hear the organ play,
And under cover of its notes
Ate through the altar's sheaf of oats.
A Low Church mouse, who thinks that I
Am too papistical, and High,
Yet somehow doesn't think it wrong
To munch through Harvest Evensong.
While I, who starve the whole year through,
Must share my food with rodents who
Except at this time of the year
Not once inside the church appear.

Within the human world I know
Such goings-on could not be so,
For human beings only do
What their religion tells them to.
They read the Bible every day
And always, night and morning, pray,
And just like me, the good church mouse,
Worship each week in God's own house,

But all the same it's strange to me
How very full the church can be
With people I don't see at all
Except at Harvest Festival.

Harvest time tells us of God's faithfulness and of his providence. 'As long as the earth remains . . . seed time and harvest shall not fail.' Once again we see before us the evidence that God has kept his promise for the harvest has again been plentiful. Year after year our heavenly Father supplies our needs. Are we truly grateful for this or do we only occasionally bother to thank him for his provision?

In our poem, the church mouse couldn't understand why some people only bother to go to church to worship at Harvest Festival. Surely God deserves a greater commitment than this?

Reading Psalm 24
Prayer No 21
Hymn 'We plough the fields and scatter'
'Thank you for every new good morning'

Candid camera

Week 5

Aim To show that God sees and cares

A car driver pulled up at the service station and, having first filled his tank with petrol, he asked the attendant to check if the engine needed more oil. Obligingly the attendant raised the bonnet of the car to discover there was no engine there at all! Obviously very puzzled by this he said, 'Excuse me, sir, but I think I should tell you there is no engine in your car!' 'Perhaps it is one of those cars with an engine at the back,' replied the driver, 'Open the boot!'

The boot was duly checked and the attendant, more bewildered than ever, said, 'I don't know how to tell you this but there *is no engine* in your car!'

At this the driver said, 'Smile, please, you're on *Candid Camera*' and he went on to explain that the producers of a popular television programme had planned the stunt. (*The name of a similar television programme may be substituted*.) The car, without an engine, had been free-wheeled downhill to the garage and there the driver had then simply applied the brakes.

Two golfers were approaching the green on a golf course. One stood by and watched as the other attempted to sink a long putt. The ball went straight into the hole but before the player could celebrate he was absolutely shocked to see a hand appear out of the hole and place the ball back on the green!

The producers of the programme *Candid Camera* had been at it again. They had made a compartment large enough to conceal a person underneath the hole. The reaction of the golfer had been recorded on film for all to see when the programme was broadcast.

An old lady put a coin in a fruit machine in an amusement

arcade. She could hardly believe what happened next. She certainly hit the jack-pot for the coins started to tumble out and kept on and on and on . . . so that she held out the bottom of her dress to try to catch them all.

She then heard the voice say, 'Smile, please, you're on *Candid Camera*'. These people were all being watched but they had no idea that they were being filmed.

What a difference it would make at school and in life generally if we all behaved as though we were being watched, as though we knew that we too, were being filmed. There would be no copying of homework, no dropping of litter, no telling lies, no stealing of pens and pencils from desks. Instead, everyone would always be kind, helpful, trustworthy, honest and considerate.

Christian application
But there is Someone who sees all that we do.

Reading Luke 12, 1–3

What a solemn thought. There is nothing hidden which will not one day be revealed. However, we must remember that as God watches over us he also loves and cares for us. He is both a loving and a forgiving Father.

Prayer No 4
Hymn 'Father lead me day by day'

Batteries

Week 6

Aim To encourage a fresh approach to studies
Visual Aid A torch battery

Today I want you to suggest some everyday things which rely upon batteries in order to work properly.

(*Compile a list such as the following*:)

Torch
Radio
Cassette recorder
Children's toys
Motor cars (to get them started)
Razors

Clocks
Smoke alarm, etc.

For each of the items you have mentioned, a battery is a source of power. None of these would function if the battery had run down. A torch would first go dim then go out altogether; a radio would go quieter, then pack in completely; clocks, razors etc. would first go slow, then stop. Batteries need replacing from time to time while certain types of battery need re-charging.

People sometimes get run down and have to have their 'batteries re-charged'. The local GP sometimes helps by giving her patient a so-called pick-me-up or a tonic. Holidays are a good opportunity to 'charge up our batteries'. We take a well-earned rest from our studies and pursue other interests at home or even take a short break to get away from it all. I hope the forthcoming half-term holiday will give you the opportunity to have some enjoyment and relaxation so that you will be able to return to school with new vigour and determination, ready for a fresh start with your batteries charged.

Christian application
Many Christian people will tell you that when they go to church to worship, to pray and to listen to God's word, it is as though they have their batteries re-charged and they are ready on the Monday to return to their work to tackle problems with new vigour. Even Jesus had to have his strength renewed. We know that occasionally he found it very helpful to go quietly on his own to pray to his Heavenly Father for strength.

Reading	Matthew 14, 22 and 23
Prayer	No 32
Hymn	'Abba, Father let me be'

Recipes

Week 7

Aim	To foster good relationships
Visual Aid	A recipe book

I've brought along my recipe book today. Try to guess what these recipes are for.

1 Ingredients: 8oz self-raising flour
Pinch salt
2oz butter or margarine
¼ pint milk
1oz caster sugar
2oz sultanas, currants or raisins.

Method: Rub the butter or margarine into the flour until like breadcrumbs, add the other ingredients and mix.

Roll out 1″ (2.5cm) thick. Cut into rounds with 2″ (5cm) cutter.
Brush surfaces with milk.
Bake in pre-heated oven at 225° (7 gas) for 10–15 minutes.
Cool on wire tray.

This is a recipe for . . . scones.

2 Now what do you think this is a recipe for?

One large portion of laziness
Add a general disinterest in work
Stir in a measure of forgetfulness
Do not add any homework
Finally, distract others from their work
Continue as above for three whole terms

As you will have guessed, this is a sure recipe for a poor report at the end of the year.

3 Here is another recipe for you to think about:

Take a country, led by a dictator with no democratic freedom for the people
To this add i) boundary disputes between nations
ii) a coveting of other nations' wealth
iii) a general inability to share the world's resources
iv) a vast stockpile of armaments
v) intolerance of other nations' cultures and religions

This, of course, is a recipe for war and for disaster on a worldwide scale. To avoid such a catastrophe, nations must learn to share the world's resources and respect one another's sovereignty.

Christian application
The following recipes can be found in the Bible:

4 This is a recipe for unhappiness and Godlessness.
Read Galatians 5, 19–21 (The 'works of the flesh')

5 But here is a wonderful recipe for the sort of life God wants us to live.
Read Galatians 5, 22–26 (The fruits of the Spirit)
6 A similar recipe can be found in the second letter of Peter, a recipe for the sort of person God wants us to be.
Read II Peter 1, 5–8

Prayer No 59
Hymn 'Make me a channel of your peace'

Who's who *Week 8*

Aim To have a goal in life
Visual Aid A copy of *Who's Who*

This massive publication is called *Who's Who*. It gives information about important people, those who hold high office, sporting personalities, pop stars, people who have achieved something notable. Here are a few extracts: (*Alternative references may, of course, be used*.)

MAJOR Rt Hon John. Conservative Member of Parliament for Huntingdon since 1983. Born 29th March 1943. Chancellor of Exchequer since 1989 until becoming Prime Minister in November 1990.

CHARLTON, Robert (Bobby Charlton) CBE 1974, OBE 1969. Director of Manchester United Football Club since 1984. Born 11th October 1937. Professional footballer with Manchester United 1954–77 for whom he played 751 games and scored 245 goals. 106 appearances for England.

RICHARD, Cliff OBE 1980. Singer and actor. Born 14th October 1940. Awarded 13 gold discs for records: 'Living Doll' 1959, 'The Young Ones' 1962, 'Bachelor Boy' 1962 . . .

RANTZEN, Esther Louise (Mrs Desmond Wilcox). Television producer and presenter since 1968. Born 22nd June 1940. Presenter of *That's Life*, *Hearts of Gold*, *Childwatch* . . .

If you become a Member of Parliament, a high official in the civil service, a high-ranking officer in the armed forces, a sports personality of renown, a well-known actor, actress or entertainer, or achieve anything which is noteworthy, your own name may one day appear in *Who's Who*. (*Mention may be made here of local dignitaries or celebrities whose names are recorded.*) This, in itself, is a very worthwhile ambition – to have your name in *Who's Who*. Remember, however, the vast majority of people are good, honest, law-abiding, hard working citizens who, though they do not become famous, make a valuable contribution to the welfare of the community.

Christian application
There is another book which is infinitely more important than *Who's Who*. It is God's book of remembrance in which he records the names of all who acknowledge and serve him (see Malachi 2, 16). In the last book of the New Testament, this is called the Lamb's Book of Life. Again it is made clear that anyone's name can be written in this book, providing they trust in God and seek to do his will (see Revelation 21, 27).

Reading Revelation 21, 22–26. John's description of the New Heaven.
Prayer No 8
Hymn 'All people that on earth do dwell'
'The Lord has need of me'

Guy Fawkes

Week 9

Aim To encourage respect for other people's points of view. To show that democracy is the best form of government for civilised people.
Visual Aid A Guy Fawkes (a group of pupils will enjoy preparing this beforehand)

As you will have noticed we have a guest at our assembly today – none other than Guy Fawkes himself. This is the time of year when we delight to have firework displays, light bonfires and burn effigies of Guy Fawkes. (I hope you will only attend properly organised bonfires and firework displays and leave the lighting of fireworks to adults. Please also read the firework code displayed on the school notice board.)

How did it all start? Why do we remember Guy Fawkes? You will no doubt think of Guy Fawkes as a traitor and a terrorist and this is certainly true for he was one of the leaders of a group of conspirators who tried to blow up King James the First and his parliament on 5th November 1605. This so-called Gunpowder Plot was discovered in the nick of time, through an anonymous letter sent to Lord Monteagle, and Guy Fawkes was discovered in the cellar beneath the Palace of Westminster, ready to fire a store of explosives. Several of the conspirators were killed and Guy Fawkes and seven others were later executed.

We tend to overlook that Guy Fawkes and the other conspirators felt they had a just cause. They did not approve of the government of the day and people of their faith were not allowed to worship as they pleased. Where they went wrong was to take the law into their own hands. It always causes tremendous suffering to innocent people when others resort to terrorism and violence. (*Reference could be made to recent atrocities brought to our attention in the news.*)

If only people would sit down and talk. If only people would discuss their differences. If only people would respect and make allowances for the points of view of other people. If only people would be prepared to accept the decisions made by democratically-elected governments. How much suffering, distress, hardship, bloodshed would be avoided! For, in a democratic society, should we disapprove of measures being taken by those who represent us, we can register our disapproval by the way we vote at the next election.

Surely the message of 5th November is that we should learn to respect other people's points of view and cherish the democracy in which we live.

Christian application

God tells us in his word that we should respect other people. We should never act hastily or condemn them out of hand. Always think before you speak or act, for you may be more at fault than the other person.

Reading	Matthew 7, 1–5 also 1 John 4, 7–11 'Let us love one another for love is of God'
Prayer	No 39 and No 41

Hymn	'Dear Lord and Father of mankind'
Chorus	'Let there be love shared among us'

The greatest sentence *Week 10*

Aim To put the message of God's love in a nutshell
An assembly suitable for Remembrance Day

I'm going to suggest to you today what is the greatest sentence which has ever been uttered. Let us first draw up a short list:

NEIL ARMSTRONG: Could the greatest sentence be the words uttered by the US astronaut, Neil Armstrong, when he became the first man to set foot on the moon in July 1969:

'That's one small step for man, one giant leap for mankind.'

P.T. BARNUM: The US showman Phineas Taylor Barnum made that shrewd statement:

'You can fool some of the people all the time, and all of the people some of the time; but you can't fool all of the people all the time.'

LAURENCE BINYON: The English poet Robert Laurence Binyon, who died in 1943, penned these famous words which are quoted every Remembrance Sunday.

'They shall grow not old, as we that are left grow old; age shall not weary them, nor the years condemn: at the going down of the sun and in the morning, we will remember them.'

RUPERT BROOKE: Another famous English poet, Rupert Brooke, wrote in his poem 'The Soldier' these much-quoted words:

'If I should die, think only this of me: that there's some corner of a foreign field that is for ever England.'

WINSTON CHURCHILL: Renowned as one of the greatest prime ministers, Winston Churchill uttered these immortal words on 20th August 1940 after the Battle of Britain:

'Never in the field of human conflict was so much owed by so many to so few.'

Most of these profound statements speak of human achievements or sacrifices, and it is appropriate that we remember the sacrifices made by countless thousands of men and women in two world wars, in Vietnam, in Korea, the Falklands, Northern Ireland and in the Gulf War. We should show our gratitude to those who in many different ways strive for peace, by doing our best to see that the world in which we live is an orderly and peaceful place.

There is one sacrifice, however, which surpasses all other. It is the gift of God's son who died that we might be forgiven. The message of God's love is summed up in one sentence in John's gospel and I suggest that this gospel-in-a-nutshell is the greatest sentence ever written.

Reading	John 3, 16 'For God so loved the world that he gave his only begotten son that whosoever believeth in him should not perish but have everlasting life.'
Prayer	No 43
Hymn	'O God our help in ages past' 'Now thank we all our God'

Barrel of bricks *Week 11*

Aim	To show that there is always someone who is worse off than we are

Have you ever experienced one of those days when everything seems to go wrong? Do you ever wonder 'Why does it always happen to me?' I want to tell you an amusing story which shows that there is always someone worse off. No one could possibly have as bad an experience as the bricklayer in this story told by Gerard Hoffnung.

This is the tragic letter written by a bricklayer from Golders Green to the firm for whom he works.

Respected Sir, When I got to the top of the building I found that the hurricane had knocked some bricks off the top, so I rigged up a beam with a pulley at the top of the building and hoisted up a couple of barrels full of bricks. When I had fixed the building there were a lot of bricks left over. I hoisted the barrel back up again and secured the line at the bottom and then went up and filled the barrel with the extra bricks. Then I went to the bottom and cast off the line. Unfortunately, the barrel of bricks was heavier than I was and before I knew what was happening the barrel started down, jerking me off the ground. I decided to hang on! Halfway up I met the barrel coming down and received a severe blow on the shoulder. I continued to the top, banging my head against the beam and getting my fingers jammed in the pulley. When the barrel hit the ground the bottom burst out, spilling all the bricks. I was now heavier than the barrel and so started down again at high speed. Halfway down I met the barrel coming up and received severe injury to my shins. When I reached the ground I landed on the broken bricks getting several painful cuts from the sharp edges. At this point I must have lost my presence of mind, because I let go of the line. The barrel then came down giving me another heavy blow and putting me in hospital. I beg to request sick leave.'

That story was, of course, made up! There are, however, always people who are worse off than we are. There is no reason to think 'Why does everything happen to me?'. No doubt we all have our share of trouble but we should take comfort from the knowledge that others have the same experiences. Instead of looking on the gloomy side, start counting all the things which have gone right, you will be surprised. Count your blessings!

Christian application
We take comfort, too, from the knowledge that Jesus knows all about our problems and our struggles and promises to be with us until the end of time. Whatever trouble we may encounter we should not hesitate to ask for God's help.

Reading	Proverbs 18, 24 and Matthew 28, 20b (also Matthew 7, 7)
Prayer	No 19 (and a prayer for the sick, No 20 or 29)
Hymn	'When upon life's billows you are tempest tossed' 'With Jesus in the boat we can smile at the storm' 'Now thank we all our God'

Footprints

Week 12

Theme	Following a good example
Visual Aids	Cards with outline footprints of some of the pupils present

I'm going to talk to you this morning about footprints. Can you guess who has made these footprints? I will give you some clues. (*Show the first card.*)

This footprint has been made by a person who is good at sport.

She plays for one of the school teams. The netball team. She is the shooter. In a recent match she scored four times. Yes, it is a footprint belonging to ——————.

The second print was made by a very tired foot. It belongs to a boy who has recently taken part in a sponsored walk. This foot walked twenty miles and helped its owner to raise . . . . . for the school charity. It belongs to ——————. (*Alternative more suitable examples may, of course, be used.*)

Both of these people have set good examples for us to follow. We should all try to follow in someone else's footsteps but at the same time try to set a good example ourselves. It is often said of a young man that he is following in his father's footsteps if, for example, he decides to follow in the same career.

In the popular Christmas carol, Good King Wenceslas tells the page that he will be alright, he will be kept safe if he follows in his master's footsteps.

Think of someone you admire and follow in their footsteps.

Christian application

Here now is a slightly different story about footprints.

One night a man had a dream, he dreamed he was walking along the beach with the Lord. Across the sky flashed scenes from his life, for each scene he noticed two sets of footprints in the sand, one belonging to him the other to the Lord.

When the last scene of his life flashed before him he looked back at the footprints in the sand; he noticed that many times along the path of his life there was only one set of footprints, he also noticed that it had happened at the very lowest and saddest times of his life.

This really bothered him and he questioned the Lord.

'Lord, you said that once I decided to follow you you'd walk with me all the way, but I have noticed that during the most troublesome times in my life there is only one set of footprints, I don't understand why when I needed you most you would leave me.'

The Lord replied, 'During your times of trial and suffering when you see only one set of footprints, it was then that I carried you!'

Jesus not only promises to be with us in all we do but is the best example of all for us to follow. 'For he is our childhood pattern.'

Reading	Isaiah 9, 2, 6 and 7 A prophecy about the coming of Jesus
Prayer	No 23
Carol	'Once in royal David's city'

Mistletoe

Week 13

Aim	To show that we should not just rely upon others but show for them a real love and concern
Visual Aid	A sprig of mistletoe (plastic if necessary)

You all know that if a young lady stands under the mistletoe she could well receive a kiss from an admirer. We look upon mistletoe as a symbol of love and affection. Let me explain why.

It was a Roman and Norse custom to decorate homes with evergreen in the middle of winter. This pagan idea was to use the foliage as a charm to ensure that warmer weather would return and bring with it new life to the earth in spring. One of the evergreens traditionally used for this purpose was mistletoe. Christians have been happy to go along with this custom of decorating their homes at Christmas time with evergreens, including mistletoe; but instead of embracing the pagan superstition they look upon mistletoe as a symbol of the love God shows for us at Christmas in the gift of his son and the love we should show for each other.

I'd like to tell you some interesting facts about mistletoe. Did you know that it is a parasite? That means that it is a plant which doesn't grow on its own, in the ground. It grows on another plant and depends on the juices of that plant for its own nourishment. In South Australia the mistletoe is a real problem, a real blight, because it grows on the branches of the gum tree and uses up the tree's supply of food, eventually causing the tree to die. Birds like to eat the mistletoe berries and then when they fly to other trees they leave the mistletoe seeds on branches. More mistletoe then springs to life. For the inhabitants of South Australia, mistletoe is a scourge.

People are sometimes like parasites! This would even apply to us if we:

- left mum to do all the housework on her own
- left our classmates to keep the classroom clean and tidy without doing our fair share
- relied on others to do the work and then just copied from them

If we behaved like this we would be like a parasite, taking advantage of someone else's kindness.

The message of the mistletoe is therefore twofold. Don't just take advantage of other people but show for them the love and concern of which we are reminded at Christmas.

Reading	Romans 12, 9–16
Prayer	No 5

Hymn 'Love came down at Christmas'
'Our eyes have seen the glory of our Saviour Christ the Lord'

Letters to Santa

Week 14

Aim To encourage generosity
Visual Aid A picture of Father Christmas

Do you recognise this person? You will, no doubt, recall writing letters to him – not many years ago!

Here are some letters which young children have written to Santa.

1 Dear Santa Claus, I want one of everything you got! John.
2 Dear Santa Claus, I need toys for this year and the next year and the next year. I can't write every year. Love Sally.
3 Dear Santa, Don't leave any presents for my brother Stephen, he doesn't deserve anything. Love Jason.
4 Dear Father Christmas, How can you tell who are the good children and who are the bad ones? I need to know as soon as possible. Ian.
5 Dear Santa, My grandmother told me that the best present is good health. Since I am already very well I would like a doll instead. Susan.
6 Dear Santa Claus, Last year you left me a space ship but I'm fed up with it! Please leave me a bike this year. Love Tom.

7 Dear Santa, Please wake me up, I want to pull your beard. Tracy.
8 Dear Father Christmas, For the last three years you haven't left me anything very good. This year is your last chance. William.

Have you noticed that most of the letters are very selfish? 'I want!' 'Please give me!' Of course they were written by very young children and it is an indication that you are growing up when you begin to think what you can give to your friends and relatives to make *their* Christmas happy.

Christian application
This is what Jesus said about giving: 'It is more blessed to give than to receive.' (see Acts 20, 35) To his disciples he said, 'Freely you have received, freely give.' This Christmas let us think not so much of what we can get but of what we can give to help others.

(*Here a mention could be made of the school's Christmas charity.*)

When we consider God's love to us in the gift of his son, our response should be one of generosity as we think of those who are less fortunate.

Reading	1 John 4, 7–12
Prayer	No 27
Hymn	'Love came down at Christmas'

The twelve days of Christmas *Week 15*

Aim	To discover what gifts we can offer
Visual Aid	A Christmas present
Audio Aid	A recording of 'The twelve days of Christmas'

I'm sure you will all be very busy now, buying presents for your parents, relatives and friends. Then when you have bought them you will carefully wrap them in Christmas paper like this.

Everyone likes to receive presents but as you grow older you will discover there is just as much pleasure in giving presents. What would you like for Christmas? Gone are the days when you would tell Father Christmas what you want! People sometimes give us presents which we don't really like but all the same, if we are polite, we will still say, 'That's just what I wanted!'

I wonder how grateful you would be if you received the gifts mentioned in the seasonal song 'The twelve days of Christmas'? Let's listen to the record. (*Alternatively read the words.*)

Perhaps the young lady who received these gifts wrote thank-you letters. If so, they could have been like these:

25th December

My dearest darling, What a lovely, romantic thought sending a partridge in a little pear tree! Bless you and thank you,

Your ever loving Emma

26th December

My dearest Albert, The two turtle doves you kindly sent this morning are sitting happily on a branch of the pear tree. I am so grateful.

With love as always, Emma

27th December

My darling Albert, What an original idea! Three French hens as a Christmas present are most unusual. Thank you all the same, I do appreciate your thoughtfulness.

Your loving Emma

28th December

Dearest Albert, What a surprise. The four calling birds arrived safely this morning. They are very sweet but they make so much noise I can't make myself heard. I expect they will quieten down when they get used to their new surroundings. I'm very grateful of course.

Love from Emma

29th December

Dearest Albert, Fancy sending five gold rings – one for each finger. I much prefer these to the birds which are taking rather a lot of looking after. Perhaps I could use the rings to 'wring' their necks! I do love the rings.

Love Emma

30th December

Dear Albert, I didn't know what to expect when I opened the front door this morning but it certainly wasn't six geese laying eggs all over the place. Frankly I hoped you had stopped sending me birds. We haven't really any room for them and they have ruined the lawn. I know you meant well.

Love Emma

31st December

Albert! I thought I said no more birds, but this morning I woke up to find no less than seven swans all trying to swim in our tiny goldfish pond. *Please stop* sending birds.

Your Emma

1st January

What do you expect me to do with eight milkmaids, and their cows? Frankly I prefer the birds. I'm afraid I no longer find this amusing.

Emma

2nd January

Now just look here, Albert, this has gone on for long enough! You call these nine people ladies? Judging by the way they are dancing round the village green they are quite shameless. The whole village is gossiping. If you value my friendship then kindly stop sending these ridiculous presents.

Emma

3rd January

As I write I can see ten old men, leaping about in what used to be our garden. The neighbours are now trying to have us evicted. I shall never speak to you again.

Emma

4th January

Right, that's it. You know very well how much I detest bagpipes. Eleven pipers are driving me mad. The council has just been round and declared our house unfit for habitation. Mother has been taken away in an ambulance. I hope you are now satisfied.

5th January

Sir. Our client Miss Emma Winterbottom instructs me to inform you that when the entire percussion section of the Liverpool Philharmonic Orchestra arrived at half-past seven this morning she had no course left open to her but to seek an injunction to prevent you sending any more gifts. I am making arrangements for the return of all livestock.

I am, Sir, Yours faithfully,
J. Snodgrass,
Solicitor-at-law

No wonder Albert's gifts weren't really appreciated. We should always give some thought to the gifts we give to people.

Christmas time is an appropriate time to give gifts, following the example of the Wise Men who brought their gifts of gold, frankincense and myrrh to the Christ child.

Is there any suitable gift we can give to our heavenly Father in return for his love to us in sending Jesus to be our Saviour? The carol we are now going to sing tells of the only gift which is suitable.

> What can I give him
> Poor as I am,
> If I were a shepherd
> I would bring a lamb.
> If I were a wise man
> I would do my part.
> Yet, what I can I give him,
> Give my heart.

We should give to God ourselves in his service and the service of others.

Carol 'In the bleak mid-winter'
Reading Matthew 2, 1–11
Prayer No 26

Year 2
Spring term

Red Riding Hood

Week 1

Aim To discourage deceit
Visual Aid Pantomime programmes or posters

Once again it is the pantomime season. (*The school may well be organising a visit or putting on a pantomime.*) How many of you intend going to the pantomime this year? They are not just for young children!

A favourite panto is *Red Riding Hood*, in which the little girl of that name is asked by her mother to take a basket of freshly baked cakes to her granny who lives in a cottage in the woods. 'Be careful to look out for dangerous wolves!' are her mother's last words as Red Riding Hood sets out. On arrival at the cottage she goes in to see her granny. Somehow, her appearance seems somewhat different, which prompts Red Riding Hood to say, 'Granny, what big eyes you've got'. This brings the familiar reply (*the children may be encouraged to join in*): 'All the better to see you with.'

Then she notices the ears and says 'But Granny, what big ears you've got'. Back comes the reply, 'All the better to hear you with!'

Finally she comments on her granny's teeth. 'And what big teeth you've got.' This time the reply is 'All the better to eat you with!'

The wolf, who had disguised himself in the granny's clothing while granny was locked in a cupboard, then springs out of bed and chases the scared Red Riding Hood out of the cottage and into the wood. All pantos have a happy ending! As luck would have it, Red Riding Hood's father, who was a wood cutter, happened to be on hand to rescue her.

The wolf in granny's clothing had attempted to deceive by pretending to be what he was not.

Do we ever do the same? Do we ever try to give others a false impression? Do we, for example, leave the music on the music stand to give our parents the impression we have done our allotted practice, or leave our homework books scattered around for the same reason?

Do we like to have all the best cricket equipment to try to give the opposition the impression that we are better cricketers than we really are? Of course, no one here would ever dream of writing big and leaving spaces in an attempt to deceive the teacher into thinking they have done a lot of work!

Next time you are tempted to be a wolf in granny's clothing

remember that your parents and your teachers are very rarely taken in by such tricks! They are more shrewd than you think.

Christian application
Though the Bible doesn't warn us about wolves in granny's clothing, it does give a clear warning about people who are wolves in sheep's clothing which is very much the same thing.

Reading	Matthew 7, 15–20
Prayer	No 42 For the New Year
Hymn	'Heavenly Father may thy blessing'

Medicine

Week 2

Theme	The cure for the world's ills
Visual Aid	A medicine bottle and spoon

You may wonder why I am holding this bottle of medicine. The reason is because I am not feeling very well. I have a sore throat, a headache, I keep sneezing, and have a troublesome cough. I've got aching limbs and keep going hot and cold. On the way to school I called at the doctor's and he prescribed this medicine and said it would help to make me better. (*Take off the cap and think about pouring a spoonful.*)

But I dislike medicine. In fact if there is one thing I hate more than being ill, it is having to take medicine. Let me see now – what does it say on the label?

'Mentholated Bronchial Balsam, extra strong for rapid relief of troublesome coughs and irritation in the throat.' Well that seems to be what I need, (*make as though you are about to pour a spoonful*) . . .

No, I'm not going to take it, I don't like medicine and anyway I haven't read the dosage.

'Shake the bottle vigorously, Dose, to be taken every 4 hours – adults two 5ml spoonfuls.' There's no way I'm going to take *two* spoonfuls. (*Replace the cap on the bottle.*)

Now if I really had been ill (and I'm not) you would think me stupid if I didn't take medicine which the doctor had prescribed. And incidentally you should *never* take medicine which has *not* been prescribed for you. It could be very dangerous to do so. But to have the remedy in your own hands and not take what has been prescribed is very stupid.

You have probably heard people say that 'This is a sick world'. When we hear of elderly people being mugged and robbed, and of harm coming to young children; when we hear of nations fighting against other nations, destroying cities and killing innocent people, then we probably agree that there is much in the world which is sick.

The good news is that we have the remedy in our own hands. (*Show the Bible.*) It is God's word. But so many people are so silly that they do not apply the remedy.

Now listen to some of the good advice and help offered in God's word as I read some verses from Psalm 119.

Reading	Psalm 119 verses 1, 9, 11, 50, 60, 72, 101, 105, 165
Prayers	No 3 and No 31
Hymn	'Lord thy word abideth'
	'They word is like a garden Lord'

Snowflakes *Week 3*

Aim	To reveal God's wonders of creation
Visual Aids	Picture of a snow scene; diagrams of snowflakes

Something young people seem to have in common is that they enjoy going out in the snow! Building snowmen, having snowball fights, tobogganing, all these add to the fun.

The next time it snows heavily I want you to go out to the field (or playground) and count how many snowflakes have fallen!

How many do you think there would be in this snow scene? There must be trillions upon trillions of snowflakes combining to make up such a beautiful scene. When you wake up in the morning and look out of your bedroom window at the snow which has fallen during the night and you see the undisturbed white carpet and every branch and twig loaded with snow you will surely be amazed at the breathtaking beauty of the scene. It is impossible to estimate how many snowflakes there are. Numbers lose all meaning. But here is an even more amazing fact.

Every single snowflake is a precise geometric pattern of exquisite beauty. They are all six-sided and have a certain 'family likeness', yet every one is different. Some are simple and star-shaped, others have many branches of fantastic detail. In general the small flakes come from very cold storms when the air holds little moisture. The more elaborate ones are seen when the air is saturated with water vapour

and the temperature only a little below freezing. You must realise of course that, when you see snowflakes falling, they are several crystals which have joined together.

Next time you look at a beautiful snow scene ponder the fact that every snow flake is a perfect and exquisite design and yet no two flakes are identical. What an amazing world we live in.

Christian application
God has demonstrated his amazing skill in the beauty and variety with which each tiny flake is formed. No wonder he said to Job when he was showing him how little Job really knew, 'Have you entered into the treasures of the snow?' (Job 38, 22) God shows the same patience and interest in every tiny detail of our lives.

Reading Matthew 10, 29–31
Prayers No 17 and No 55
Hymn 'In the bleak mid-winter'

Waste not, want not *Week 4*

Aim To foster a greater awareness of the need to recycle
Visual Aids A pile of newspapers and comics, a glass bottle, a plastic container and drink can

The old proverb 'Waste not, want not' has taken on a new meaning. Originally it simply encouraged families to be economical. If you throw away food or other commodities just because you have sufficient for your use it would indeed be wasteful, because you need not have bought so much in the first place. Putting unwanted food in the bin, for example, is just throwing away money.

The proverb has now taken on a world-wide significance. Industry is now producing such a vast quantity of goods that if countries do not stop wasting their resources they will, in the foreseeable future, run out of resources. The answer to this universal problem is to recycle – that means rather than destroy used material we should re-process it and use it all over again. A group of pupils will now tell us which materials can be recycled and why it is essential that this should be done.

1ST PUPIL: **Paper** Almost all paper comes from conifer and eucalyptus trees which are farmed for this purpose. If we use recycled paper more trees will be saved. This will help to save the natural wildlife habitats in places like the Scottish Highlands and other timber-producing countries. Only 30 per cent of the paper and cardboard we use in the United Kingdom is recycled. One problem to be overcome is to persuade people to buy items made from recycled paper. They are reluctant to do so because they think it is poor quality. This is surely a minor consideration when we compare it with the vast saving of the world's resources of timber.

2ND PUPIL: **Glass** It is bad enough when we see empty bottles left lying on waste ground or on the streets, but think of the danger to children when broken bottles are left on beaches and playing fields. How much safer it would be to put empty bottles in the special bottle banks provided by most local authorities. What a saving, too, because glass can be recycled. 6,000 million glass containers are used in the United Kingdom each year but it is thought that only 17 per cent is recycled. What a waste!

3RD PUPIL: **Plastic** How unsightly our towns and countryside are made by people throwing away plastic containers. Nearly half the packaging used in Britain is made out of plastic. Unfortunately, plastic cannot easily be burned. As yet scientists have not discovered a successful way of giving plastic a second life but since plastic is made from one of the world's most valuable resources, oil, which one day will run out, it is vital that a way is found to recycle it.

4TH PUPIL: **Cans** During the Second World War people realised how important it was to recycle metal. Iron railings surrounding parks and private houses were removed, the metal melted down and made into armaments. How wasteful people have become since then, throwing away items like drinks cans when they could well be recycled. Many manufacturers are now helping by introducing, on their products, symbols saying whether the can is made of aluminium or tin-plated steel so that collecting is made easier.

Can you think of other ways in which we can avoid wastage?

1 Turn off all unwanted lights
2 Never leave taps running
3 Use up all the space in exercise books
4 Always close doors to keep the heat in

If we do all these things we shall save ourselves money in the long run. Waste not, want not.
(*This assembly could be used to launch a money-raising project for either school funds or charity, by collecting newspapers, cans, etc.*)

Christian application
God's word tells us that there are other valuable commodities which we should not waste, namely *time* and *talents*. Jesus was aware how short time is and how valuable. That is why he said, 'I must work the works of him that sent me while it is day, the night comes when no man can work'. In one of the stories he told he made it quite clear that God is displeased if we waste the talents he has given us.

Reading	Matthew 25, 14–30 We must not squander our God-given opportunities.
Prayer	No 17 and No 51
Hymn	'Awake my soul and with the sun' 'This is the day that the Lord has made'

Yes–No interlude *Week 5*

Aim	To develop a sense of values
Visual Aid	A gong

One of the earliest quiz programmes to be televised, long before your time, had what was called a *Yes–No* interlude. The idea was that competitors took a turn at being interviewed by the compere. If they managed to avoid using the words 'Yes' or 'No' for a whole minute they won a small prize; but if they used either of those words then the gong was sounded to show that they had lost.

(*Select a couple of suitable 'volunteers' to help with the demonstration and proceed to ask each, in turn, a series of questions. The following trick questions may be used to catch them out.*)

TEACHER: Now are you ready for me to ask you some questions?
PUPIL: Yes. (*Sound gong.*)
TEACHER: Just relax now and tell me your name.
PUPIL: Sally.
TEACHER: Sorry, I didn't catch it, did you say Sarah?
PUPIL: No – Sally. (*Gong.*)
TEACHER: You didn't say 'no' then did you?
PUPIL: No. (*Gong.*)

In that game competitors have to learn *not* to say 'Yes' and *not* to say 'No'. In life we have to learn *when* to say 'Yes' and *when* to say 'No'.

(*Volunteers may be called for here.*)

'Will you hold the door open please?' (Answer – 'Yes.')

'Will you try to keep your bedroom tidy?' (Answer – 'Yes.')

'Will you help to sell tickets for the school play?' (Answer – 'Yes.')

'Will you help to put away the games equipment?' (Answer – 'Yes.')

'I'm going to skip games to-day, the teacher won't notice. Will you come with me?' (Answer – 'No.')

'I'm not going to bother going to the choir rehearsal to-day. Will you give it a miss too?' (Answer – 'No.')

'I didn't have time to do my homework, will you let me copy yours?' (Answer – 'No, I'm sorry that would not be fair!')

Don't be tempted by others to do what you know is wrong. Learn to say 'No'.

When you are asked to lend a helping hand, don't just leave it to someone else. Learn to say 'Yes'.

Christian application

God's word makes it clear that life itself is full of choices, that we have to learn when to say 'Yes' and when to say 'No'. Many of the people Jesus invited to follow him said 'No' (Matthew 19, 22); and others gave up when the going got tough (John 6, 66). What is our response to Jesus' invitation 'Come follow me'? I hope it is, 'Yes, I will follow you'.

Reading	Luke 5, 27 and 28. Matthew's response to the Lord's invitation.
Prayer	No 36
Hymn	'I have decided to follow Jesus' 'Follow, follow, I would follow Jesus'

Have a heart *Week 6*

Aim	To encourage sympathy and understanding
Visual Aid	A Valentine card depicting a heart

Have you received one of these? (*Show card.*) More about that later. The incidents I'm about to describe all contain well-used sayings which have one word in common.

1 Mum was trying to get the tea ready, the kettle was boiling, there was a knock on the front door, the telephone started to ring, and when Jane said, 'Will you help me with my homework?' Mum replied, 'Have a heart, I can't do everything at once!'
2 Albert was always grumbling about the weather, politics, the local council. Perhaps it was because he was getting on in years and lived on his own. But those who knew him well said that he would do anything to help, that 'his heart was in the right place'.
3 Susan wondered who on earth would have sent her a Valentine card and when she opened it the anonymous sender had written, 'I love you with all my heart!'
4 There had been a power failure. It was very dark as John fumbled and searched for a torch. The wind was howling round the corner of the house. Suddenly the casement window blew open. John's heart started to beat faster and faster.

How strange, isn't it, that we should refer to the heart in so many different ways? After all it is only a pump which sends blood round the body. But it is a vital organ for it sustains life. That is why people think of it as a symbol of life itself.

When people are mourning the loss of a loved one it is right that we send our heartfelt sympathies to them. If friends are in trouble or are going through a particularly anxious time we should have the heart to tell them that we are prepared to do anything we can to help.

When Valentine's Day comes round, the *heart* features in many of the messages we send or receive, for the heart is a symbol of love, sympathy and understanding.

Christian application
The heart is mentioned many times in the Bible. It means 'our whole being' or 'our real self'. Here are some references for you to think about.

Reading 1 Samuel 16, 7. God looks on the heart.
Psalm 44, 21. God knows the secrets of the heart.
Romans 10, 10. With the heart man believes.
Deuteronomy 13, 3. Love the Lord with all your heart.
Psalm 86, 12. I will praise thee O Lord with all my heart.
Proverbs 3, 5. Trust in the Lord with all your heart.
Ephesians 3, 17. That Christ may dwell in your hearts by faith.

Prayer No 38 or No 39 or No 5 (depending on circumstances)
Hymn 'Thou didst leave thy throne'
Chorus 'He lives!'

Railways

Week 7

Theme Learning to control your temper
Visual Aid A model steam engine or a poster of a steam locomotive

Have you ever been to a model railway exhibition? If so then I wonder if you could get near any of the exhibits, or was your view blocked by all the adults who were there? Even in toy shops you may find notices near the model trains 'These are not toys, they are collectors' models!'.

This fascination for steam locomotives is due to a nostalgia for a bygone age. It is difficult for us who live in the age of the supertanker and supersonic jet airliner to appreciate the impact of railways in the nineteenth century. For the thirty years from 1830 to 1860 Britain was gripped by railway mania. Every town, port and village had to have a railway. As the nineteenth century progressed, steam trains were made more comfortable but the most significant advancement was the speed at which they could travel. The line from London to Aberdeen is historically important for it was along a stretch of this line – between Perth and Montrose – that attempts were made at the speed record. Drivers were frequently carried shoulder-high from their steaming engines by cheering colleagues after a record run had been made.

But steam engines were cumbersome brutes which took hours of preparation and stoking before they could raise sufficient steam to begin a journey, pulling either passenger train or goods wagons. An express locomotive of the 1880s guzzled a hundredweight of coal every three miles and used up to thirty gallons of water every mile. Allowing for the initial warm-up, for starts and stops, a fireman had to shovel three tons of coal from tender to fire box on a run from London to York or London to Crewe. But once the engine was steamed up, what power could be unleashed.

Alas, it was a bad crash of the Scots Flyer at Preston in July 1896 which put an end to attempts on the speed record for many years. However, the LNER locomotive 'Mallard' gained the existing record of 126 mph on 3rd July 1938. This is one record which is likely to stand for all time as steam locomotives were replaced by the more commercial diesel engines in the 1960s.

The fascination of steam lures families to give up their weekends restoring old locomotives. What a thrill it gives them when their task is complete and once again they are able to see the old engine getting steamed up.

People, too, get 'steamed up'. Have you ever seen someone get so angry that they start blustering, get very red in the face and often let their fists fly? Too many people act first and think afterwards. It doesn't need to take them hours to get steamed up! How much better it would be for all concerned, when others provoke and say unkind things, if we could just count to ten, try to control our temper and think first of the consequences of violent action.

Christian application
Jesus tells his followers not to get 'steamed up' – well not in so many words. Listen now to what he says.

Reading Luke 6, 27–36

Prayer No 9
Hymn 'Heavenly Father may thy blessing'

One way

Week 8

Theme Keeping on the straight and narrow
Visual Aid A road sign, as illustrated

Do you recognise this road sign? It has a white arrow on a blue background. It indicates a one-way street and instructs traffic to travel in the direction of the arrow.

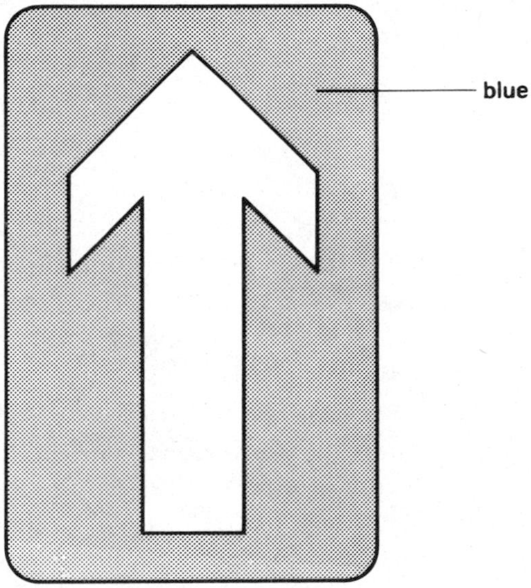

Should a motorist inadvertently find him or herself travelling in the wrong direction in a one-way street, she or he could well meet on-coming traffic. The result would be a disaster.

We do well to make sure that we are travelling in the right direction as we journey through life.

There is one way for a sports team to ensure success. It is for every member to be fully committed, to train hard and to put in a lot of practice.

There is one way to ensure success with our studies. It is to concentrate on our work, to give of our best effort, in other words to be conscientious.

There is, conversely, one way which leads to disappointment. It is to be inattentive, to be careless, thoughtless and generally uninterested.

Christian application
There is one way which surely leads to God's heavenly kingdom. It is to be followers of Jesus Christ for he said, 'I am the way, the truth and the life, no man comes to the Father but by me'.

Not only is the Christian way 'one-way only', it is also described as a narrow way from which we must not allow ourselves to be diverted.

Reading	Matthew 7, 7–14
Prayer	No 23
Hymn	'Follow, follow, I would follow Jesus'
	'One more step along the world I go'

Door signs

Week 9

Aim	To show what our response to God's love should be
Visual Aids	Five notices: **Private**, **Wait**, **No Unauthorised Person Admitted**, **Enter**, **Please Knock**

Where are we likely to see these signs? If you have been observant you will have noticed them around this building. They are signs which are frequently found on doors. A room with **Private** on the door means that you can't go in to that room because it belongs to some special person. You may only go in if invited to do so. If you see this notice . . . (*hold up* **Please Knock**), then you may knock and wait to see if you are invited to go in. The person inside has every right to his or her privacy and may not be quite ready to see you. Some rooms have a special illuminated instruction above the door telling you to **Wait**. When it is convenient for you to be seen this instruction can be changed to the invitation **Enter**.

Most people don't like gate crashers, that is people forcing their way in uninvited. We only like people who have been invited coming into our homes or onto our premises. For this reason premises often display the notice **No Unauthorised Person Admitted**.

God's word teaches that there is an imaginary door into a person's life. Of course we ourselves are entitled to privacy and may hang the **Private** sign on our life's door for we resent it when other people interfere, especially if they are uninvited. We have the right to say that 'No unauthorised person' will be admitted to our lives.

John, in the book of the Revelation, uses this illustration to show that Jesus is knocking on the door of our lives, asking if he can come in to help us and guide us. It would be very unwise if we rudely put up a 'Keep out' sign, or even told him to 'Wait'. Our response to God's love should be to ask Jesus to come in to our lives as our friend and saviour.

On the door of our lives should be the word '**Enter**', asking Jesus to be our Lord.

Reading	Revelation 3, 19–22
Prayer	No 22
Hymn	'Thou didst leave thy throne'

A blind eye *Week 10*

Aim	To show that occasionally it is acceptable to turn a blind eye
Visual Aid	A telescope

There can be few visitors to London who have not seen Nelson's Column in Trafalgar Square. This monument to Viscount Horatio Nelson quite rightly has this prominent place in the city, for Lord Nelson was one of the greatest British admirals. As a result of wounds sustained in sea battles he lost the sight of his right eye in 1794 and lost his right arm in 1797. Undeterred by these injuries he continued to pursue enemy fleets which threatened our nation and he became a national hero. His greatest victory was the defeat of the combined French and Spanish fleets off Cape Trafalgar, twenty enemy ships being captured. Sadly in this engagement Lord Nelson was mortally wounded on board his flagship 'Victory'.

Nelson was never one to flee from danger. On one occasion he was told of the approach of enemy ships and that it would perhaps be prudent to get out of the area. He then put his telescope to his blind eye and uttered those famous words, 'I see no ships!'. From this incident we derive the well-known saying 'to turn a blind eye'. It means that we choose to overlook something and pretend that it has never happened or doesn't exist.

Here is a story which may be familiar to you. It was time for the class to hand in their homework books but James hadn't done his. All the class were waiting to see what the teacher would say because he had warned them that failure to hand in homework on time would incur a severe penalty. They felt sure that James would have to stay behind after school for at least an hour. But on this occasion the teacher surprised them all by saying, 'I know, James, that in your case there are special circumstances, your mother is very ill and you are having to look after your two younger sisters and baby brother. In view of this I am prepared to turn a blind eye to it.'

We should always be prepared to make allowances for the actions of other people when we know there are special circumstances.

Christian application
It doesn't ever serve any useful purpose to retaliate when people say unkind things about us or even do things to offend us. Remember always that we can't very well ask God to forgive us for what we have done wrong if we are not prepared to forgive others.

Reading	Matthew 18, 21–35
Prayer	No 19
Hymn	'Make me a channel of your peace'

A blind spot *Week 11*

Aim	To show that it is often wise to be aware of our limitations
Visual Aid	A card with a black spot and a cross

When you have a spare moment I want you to carry out a little experiment. On a sheet of paper draw a round black spot and also, about 10cm to the right, a small, black cross. Now close your left eye and hold the sheet directly in front of you at arms length. Gradually bring it nearer to your face. Keep your right eye firmly on the round spot as you do so. Without taking your eye off the spot you will be able to see the cross out of the corner of your eye. Suddenly, as the sheet gets nearer to your eye, the cross will disappear and only the spot will be visible. Bring the paper a little closer and the cross will re-appear. This experiment demonstrates a natural phenomenon – that we all have a blind spot.

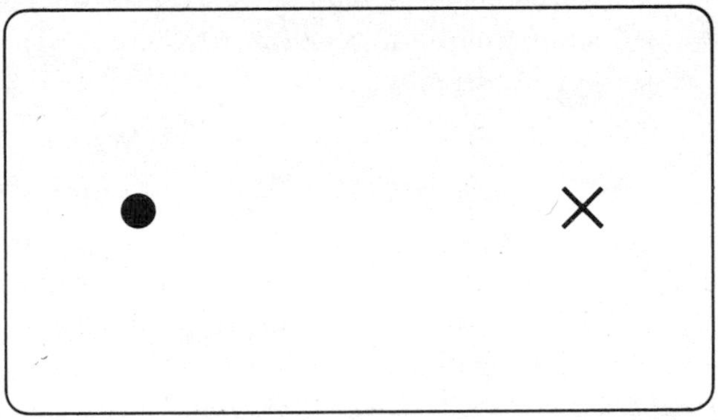

People may be said to have a blind spot if they are not very good at a particular task. You may be said to have a 'blind spot' if you are not good at maths or at art or at sport. You would think some have a blind spot when it comes to washing the dishes, or keeping their bedrooms tidy. Here at school I can't help noticing that a few people seem to have a blind spot when there is litter to be picked up or doors to be closed. What is your blind spot?

As demonstrated in our experiment, a real blind spot cannot be avoided. We can, however, overcome some of these other blind spots if we apply ourselves diligently to the tasks we are given.

Christian application
It is a fact that some people have a 'blind spot' as far as God is concerned. They find it difficult to believe in him, but the Lord will even help us to believe if we ask him. Here is a story about a man who had difficulty believing and who brought his son, who suffered from epilepsy, to Jesus to be healed.

Reading Mark 9, 17–27. 'Lord, help my unbelief.'
Prayer No 18
Hymn 'Fight the good fight'

Badges *Week 12*

Theme Showing that we belong
Visual Aids Numerous pictures of badges of clubs and societies
Pupils could be asked to bring in any badges they have to form an exhibition.
Note: This assembly is suitable for a festival service or form

assembly. Pupils may be rehearsed to read or recite the various parts. For a shorter assembly the presenter should be selective.

PRESENTER: The theme of our service is badges. We all like to belong to a club or society and, to show that we belong, we wear a badge.

1ST PUPIL: The members of form . . . have arranged an exhibition of badges which we hope you will look at when you have a moment to spare. The exhibits include the following badges:
AA (Automobile Association)
RAC (Royal Automobile Club)
YMCA (Young Men's Christian Association)
YHA (Youth Hostel Association)
Porpoise Club
National Trust
Rotary Club – a philanthropic society of business and professional people founded in 1905, now with a membership of more than 750,000
SAGA Club – organises holidays for the elderly
RSPB (Royal Society for the Protection of Birds)
YOC (Young Ornithologists' Club)
PDSA (People's Dispensary for Sick Animals, Juniors Club)
RSPCA (Royal Society for the Prevention of Cruelty to Animals)
World Wildlife Fund
Young People's Trust for Endangered Species
Sussex Trust for Nature Conservation
Greenpeace
RNLI (Royal National Lifeboat Institution)
The Guide Dogs for the Blind Association – founded in 1931
The Boys' Brigade – their badge features an anchor and the motto 'Steadfast and Sure'
WRVS (Women's Royal Voluntary Service)
British Red Cross
Scouts
Guides
The St. John Ambulance
Scripture Union
Your grandparents could even have worn a badge to show that they belonged to the 'Desperate Dan Pie Eaters' Club'!

(*This is only a specimen list and would have to be varied according to available resources. For additional information see 'The Official Badge Collectors Guide' by Frank R. Setchfield, pub. Longman.*)

2ND PUPIL: Many badges appropriately depict animals.
The Porpoise Club badge features the porpoise which is the smallest of the whale family. It is appropriate because the children belonging to this club are learning to become proficient swimmers.

The Busy Bees is the junior club of the PDSA. It has an emblem of a bee.

You will be familiar with the badge which has a picture of a panda. It is used by the World Wildlife Fund and the Panda Club – associations dedicated to the preservation of wildlife and endangered species.

The emblem of the RSPB is the Avocet. This bird was re-established as a breeding bird in this country, particularly in East Anglia, thanks to the work of the RSPB.

See if you can discover other conservation organisations such as the Sussex Trust for Nature Conservation with its emblem of a butterfly.

3RD PUPIL: The National Trust is a British organisation, committed to the preservation of land and buildings of historic interest or beauty. It was founded in 1895 and now owns hundreds of historic houses, nearly half a million acres of the finest countryside and over 400 miles of unspoilt coastline. The Trust thus helps to preserve the nation's heritage for future generations. The distinctive badge or emblem of the National Trust is an oak leaf.

4TH PUPIL: Military badges have a special fascination for many people. Before the eighteenth century, regiments were simply distinguished by the name of their commanding officer. Each had its own distinctive badge. These usually incorporated the coat of arms of the commanding officer or colonel.

In 1751 a standard system of identifying regiments was introduced. Infantry regiments were given a number and were allowed to have badges which incorporated special authorized designs. Symbols, such as the Prince of Wales' Feathers, the white horse or the dragon were in common use and have remained to the present day. Mottoes were also incorporated in the badges, the most common at that time being *Nec Espera Terrent* (meaning Nor do Difficulties Deter). (*Note for teacher: From the following list select two or three examples.*)

Well known military badges include:

The Norfolk Regiment badge which bears the inscription – '*Honi Soit Qui Mal Y Pense*' meaning 'Evil to him who thinks evil'.

The badge of the Middlesex Regiment also has the same inscription, as do several others.

The Royal Artillery badge appropriately depicts a gun.

The Welsh Guards cap badge, worn from 1915, the date when the regiment was formed, bears the words '*Cymru am Byth*' which means 'Wales for Ever'.

The Army Air Corp badge, worn from 1942 to 1950 depicts an eagle. It is unusual in that it is made of hall-marked silver". Most military badges are brass or white metal.

The Royal Army Ordnance Corps 1947 to 1949 badge has three cannons.

The Buffs, East Kent Regiment 1896 to 1961 badge depicts a dragon.

The Army Educational Corps 1927 to 1946 appropriately has an open book on its badge.

The badge of the South Nottinghamshire Hussars 1908 to 1952 consists simply of oak leaves and an acorn.

The 17th Duke of Cambridge's Own Lancers NCO's badge shows a skull and cross bones with the inscription 'or glory'.

The Tank Corp formed in 1917 became the Royal Tank Corp in 1922. Its badge, as you would expect, depicts a tank. The motto is 'Fear Nought'. There are two versions of the badge with tanks facing in opposite directions.

There are many Irish regiments which have harps featured prominently on their badges:

The Royal Irish Rifles 1913 to 1952 (later became the Royal Ulster Rifles)

The Royal Irish Rangers 1968

The North Irish Horse

The 8th Irish Battalion, the Kings 1908 to 1921.

(*For further information see 'Badges of the British Army 1820 to the Present' by F. Wilkinson, Pub. Arms and Armour Press.*)

5TH PUPIL: The badge of the Metropolitan Police Force is also very distinctive. It is a star-shaped badge surmounted by a crown. In the centre are the letters E II R denoting the reign of Queen Elizabeth II. In the UK there are 56 autonomous police forces, generally organised on a county basis though they all help each other when there are special circumstances.

It was in 1829 that London's Bow Street Runners were replaced by the first London Police Force. This all happened due to the influence of the Prime Minister of the day, Robert Peel. Have you ever wondered why policemen are sometimes called Bobbies? It was after the name of the Prime Minister who established the first police force.

Nowadays different police forces have their own special badges. The badge of the Merseyside Police for example incorporates the Liver Bird from which Liverpool gets its name.

6TH PUPIL: All sports clubs have their own badges. Here, for example, are details of the badges of first-class county cricket clubs.

(*Note for teacher: Again selection will be necessary in this section. Perhaps a pupil with artistic talent could make a large illustration of the local County Cricket team's badge.*)

Derbyshire – A rose and crown
Essex – Three Seaxes
Glamorgan – Gold Daffodil
Gloucestershire – The coat of arms of the city and county of Bristol which pictures a castle on a cliff and a galleon
Hampshire – Tudor rose and crown
Kent – White horse on a red ground
Lancashire – A red rose
Leicestershire – A gold running fox on a green ground
Middlesex – Three Seaxes
Northamptonshire – The county badge of Nottinghamshire
Somerset – The Somerset Dragon
Surrey – Prince of Wales Feathers
Sussex – County arms of six Martlets
Warwickshire – A bear and ragged staff
Worcestershire – A shield with three pears
Yorkshire – A white Rose
Durham – A shield with four lions.

In 1992 Durham became the 18th first-class county team. They were given this status after their prolonged success in the minor counties championships. It had been 71 years since the last county, Glamorgan, had received this recognition.

(*For pictures of these badges and further information see 'The Guinness Book of Cricket facts and feats' by Bill Frindall.*)

PRESENTER: You have just heard (*pupil's name*) tell you a little about the badges of county cricket teams. The highest achievement for any sportsman or sportswoman is to represent their country in their chosen sport. It is a very proud moment when a person wears the national badge or emblem for the first time.

Now, this is your chance to take part in our assembly. I would like you to put up your hand if you know which countries have the following emblems:

Thistle	(Scotland)
Maple Leaf	(Canada)
Red Rose	(England)
Leek	(Wales)
Shamrock	(Ireland)
Spray of Wattle	(Australia)
Fern Frond	(New Zealand)
Lotus Flower	(Egypt)
Pomegranate	(Spain)

Many countries also use animals as their emblems. Which countries do you associate with the following:

Lion	(England)
Dragon	(Wales)
Kangaroo	(Australia)
Crowing Cock	(France)
Beaver	(Canada)
Springbok	(South Africa)
Bald Eagle	(USA)
Kiwi	(New Zealand)

7TH PUPIL: I would like to tell you about the St John Ambulance. You will all know that we carry out important work at football matches and other public functions where we are frequently called upon to administer first aid. Ours is an ancient organisation. Legend has it that in 1023 some merchants of Amalfi, an Italian republic, purchased the site in Jerusalem of an old hostel previously established by Charlemagne, and built a hospital there for the benefit of Christian pilgrims. By 1113, because of the dedication of those staffing this hospital in helping the poor and the sick, the Order of the Hospital of St John of Jerusalem was

officially established, and as a mark of recognition for the previous aid given by the Amalfi merchants, the badge of that republic, the eight-pointed white cross was adopted.
This is our badge:

8TH PUPIL: Football clubs also have their own special badges. These are the badges of some famous clubs.

Aston Villa was formed in 1873 by a group of cricketers who wanted to play soccer in the winter.

Manchester United was only formed in 1902 after their predecessors, Newton Heath, went bankrupt.
Manchester City was formed in 1894 after their predecessors, Ardwick, went bankrupt.
Everton was originally formed in 1878 by members of St Domingo Church and Sunday School.
Tottenham Hotspurs was also formed from an older cricket club and most founder members were old boys of St John's Presbyterian School and Tottenham Grammar School.
Liverpool. But for a dispute between Everton football club and their landlord at Anfield in 1892 there may never have been a Liverpool FC. The dispute caused the majority of Evertonians to leave Anfield and form the new club at Goodison Park.
Arsenal was formed by the workers at the Royal Arsenal, Woolwich, in 1886. The club was first called the Woolwich Reds then the Woolwich Arsenal. They are now nicknamed The Gunners.
Nottingham Forest is one of the oldest football clubs in the world, formed at a meeting in 1865.

9TH PUPIL: Religious organisations often have badges for their members to wear. This badge can be worn by people who are linked with Scripture Union. It depicts a lamp because Scripture Union encourages people to read the Bible regularly, and God's word, in the words of the Psalm, is 'A lamp to my feet and a light to my path' (Psalm 119: 105).

10TH PUPIL: You may also have heard of the Gideons, an organisation of Christian professionals and business people who distribute God's word by giving copies of the Bible to hotels, hospitals, prisons, schools, etc. They are called Gideons after the man in the Old Testament story and their badge consists of a white pitcher with a red flame, symbolising the jars in which Gideon's men hid their flaming torches. The gold circle represents the trumpets which Gideon's men sounded.

(*Note*: *The local branch of Gideons International could be invited to come into school to present copies of the New Testament to first year/year seven pupils*.)

11TH PUPIL: Many badges are simply a mark of membership of a club or society. Here at school you may belong to any of the following clubs or societies (*A suitable list may be read*):

Chess Club
Junior Scientific Society
Art Club
Music Society
Junior Choir
Junior Christian Society
Rounders Club
Tennis Club
Badminton Club
Cricket Club
Rugby Club, etc.

If you are a member you are entitled to wear the badge.

12TH PUPIL: Some badges indicate the status of the wearer; for example, 'Rounders Captain', 'Prefect', or 'Form Captain'. Each of these is a responsible job and the people appointed have the status of being allowed to wear a badge.

Badges are often sold in order to raise money for well-known charities like Save the Children, Help the Aged, Barnados. You may wear one of these badges if you have made your contribution.

13TH PUPIL: There is one badge which all the pupils here should wear with pride. It is the school badge. (*Here describe the school emblem and the school motto, eg* Non sibi sed omnibus – Not for one, but for all.)

You must also wear this badge with a sense of responsibility. You belong to a fine school and are proud of it. Others see that you belong because they recognise your badge and they will judge our school by your actions and behaviour. We should all see to it that we do nothing to tarnish the school's good name.

Christian application

As we conclude our festival service there is just one more badge to which I must refer, the most important badge of all. It is the badge of Christian discipleship. This badge cannot be bought in a shop or pinned to a blazer but it can be seen by everyone.

Jesus said, 'By this shall all men know that you are my disciples if you have love for one another'. Love is the badge of Christian discipleship. If we follow Jesus, who loved us so much that he died for us, then we ought also to love one another. People will see that we belong to him if we have a genuine concern and love for other people.

Reading	John 13, 31–35
Prayer	No 11 and/or No 22
Hymn	'Bind us together Lord'
	'Who is on the Lord's side?'

Triumphal entry

Week 13

Theme	Christ's triumphal entry into Jerusalem
Audio Aid	Recording of 'Entry of the gladiators' or 'When the saints go marching in' or any other music played when the local football team takes the field

I want to talk to you today about the triumphal entry. What thoughts have just passed through your mind? Which triumphal entry are we going to hear about?

Maybe you assumed I was meaning the triumphal entry of the . . . . football team. The music just played is that which heralds the arrival of the team on to the pitch when the match is about to start. (*Here reminisce about great local heroes past and present.*)

Perhaps you may have thought I was referring to the triumphant homecoming of the FA Cup winners or the winners of the Football League. On these occasions it is usual for many thousands of fans to line the streets to greet the victorious team.

Could it be that I was referring to the ticker-tape parade occasionally staged in New York? When an outstanding achievement is being recognised, such as the first landing on the moon, the heroes drive in an open-topped car through the streets of New York while they are showered with streams of paper cuttings from the machines in the offices in the skyscrapers which line the streets. It is a man-made snowstorm and a real triumphal entry.

You may even have made a triumphal entry yourself when you returned home and announced, 'Listen, everyone, I'm playing for the school tennis team on Saturday' or, 'I've had some great news, I've just been given a commendation for my geography project'.

True! All these are triumphal entries. But they are not the one to which I refer this morning. Of course you have guessed by now which it is. Let me read to you the story of a most amazing triumphal entry.

Reading Mark 11, 1–10
Jesus, God's Son, rode into Jerusalem on the most humble of beasts, an ass. By this he showed that he was coming in peace. Alas, those fickle people who gave him such a rousing reception shouting, 'Hosanna! Blessed is he who comes in the name of the Lord', were soon to change their chant to 'Crucify him! Crucify him!' Even this was part of God's marvellous plan. 'He died that we might be forgiven, he died to make us good.'

Prayer No 15

Hymn 'Hallelu, hallelu, hallelu, hallelujah
We'll praise the Lord'
'All glory, laud and honour'
'Ride on! ride on in majesty'

Year 2
Summer term

No U-turn

Week 1

Aim To encourage persistence and perseverance as we serve the risen Christ and follow his example

Visual Aid The road sign for 'No U-turn'

It is a rule that, if you find yourself travelling on a motorway in the wrong direction, you can't just turn round and go back; you have to leave at the next junction and enter the motorway from the other direction. But on other roads like busy trunk roads it may appear to be safe to make a U-turn. You have to take note therefore whether there is a sign like this one. (*Show diagram of road sign.*) This sign forbids U-turns.

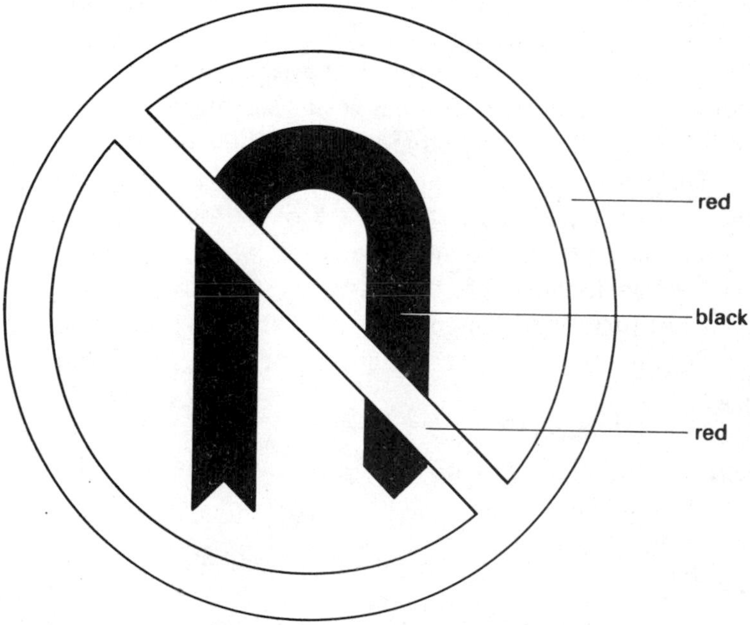

In life U-turns are often made when a person discovers that he or she has been going in the wrong direction, though some people are too stubborn to admit that they have been wrong.

Jonah was told by God to go to Nineveh to tell the people there that God was very displeased with them. But he was too scared and instead boarded a ship to sail in the opposite direction to Tarshish. The story of how God over-ruled in his life and helped him to make a U-turn is told in the book of Jonah in the Old Testament.

Thomas didn't believe the other disciples when they told him that

Jesus had risen from the dead and that they had all seen him. But Thomas persisted in his disbelief and said he would need to see the imprint of the nails in Jesus' hands for himself. It was when Jesus appeared to the disciples for the second time that Thomas was with them. He exclaimed 'My Lord and my God'. His faith had undergone a U-turn.

Perhaps the greatest U-turn recorded in the Bible was that of Saul of Tarsus, a devout Jewish leader, who was so intent on persecuting the Christians for spreading what he thought was a lie about the resurrection, that he went to Damascus, with a warrant for their arrest. Here is what happened.

Reading Acts 9, 1–9

Saul of Tarsus then became known as Paul the apostle, a leader of the early Christian Church.

If we know that we are going in the right direction then we do well to persevere and persist. Indeed Jesus encourages us to do just that. He even warns those who start to follow him that they must not turn back. He gave them this illustration to help them to understand: 'A farmer who ploughs his field must look straight ahead all the time. Should he keep turning round the result of his ploughing would be a real mess.' Jesus said, 'He that puts his hand to the plough and turns back is not fit for the Kingdom of Heaven'. When we start to follow Jesus we are heading in the right direction. There must be no U-turns.

Prayer No 44

Hymn 'I have decided to follow Jesus,
No turning back'

Toe the line

Week 2

Aim To show that there are times when it is best to conform

Visual Aids A set of darts, a tennis ball, a shot, discus, javelin and a cricket bat

You see before you today items of equipment used in several different sports: darts, tennis, putting the shot, throwing the discus, throwing the javelin and cricket.

The question is, what do they all have in common? (*Consider the suggestions made.*) These sports all involve the participant standing on or behind a line. Darts players would have an unfair advantage if they stepped in front of the line marked on the floor and got too close to the board. Servers in tennis would be foot-faulted if they stepped over the service line because this would give a better chance of serving an ace. A batsman in a game of cricket could be stumped out if he missed the ball and both his feet were in front of the batting crease. The shot, the discus and the javelin must be delivered without the competitors' feet crossing the line. All these sporting men and women must learn to *toe the line*. If they do not they will be contravening the rules and will incur a penalty.

In many different situations in life we have to toe the line, even though it is an imaginary line. For our own sakes and for the good of others we have to observe the agreed rules.

The laws of the land are there for everyone's benefit. The police have the difficult, unenviable task of seeing to it that everyone toes the line. In education, teachers and pupils alike have to do what is expected of them. Like a tennis player if we do not toe the line we will be faulted.

Of course we try not to have unnecessary rules, but those we have are essential. Pause to think for a few moments about some of the school rules. You will surely agree that all the rules are for our wellbeing. (*Here one or two examples could be quoted.*)

Christian application

This is what the Bible says we should do if we think someone is not toeing the line.

Reading	Matthew 18, 10–15
Prayer	No 4
Hymn	'Make me a channel of your peace'

Apprentice devils *Week 3*

Aim	To discourage procrastination
Visual Aid	A card with the word **Procrastination**

Our story today is an ancient fable. One day the chief of devils was briefing three apprentice devils prior to sending them to the world in order to ruin people's lives. He questioned them about the methods they would adopt. To the first he said, 'What will you say to the people on earth?'. The apprentice replied, 'I will tell people that there is no God'. 'You won't achieve much by that,' said the chief of devils, 'For people know in their heart of hearts that there is a God!' Then turning to the next apprentice he asked, 'And what will be your technique?' 'I will tell people that there is no hell,' replied the second apprentice. 'You won't accomplish much by that approach either, for people look around them, see so much evil and destruction, and know there must be a hell,' commented the chief. Finally, he asked the third apprentice what he would do. 'I will simply tell men that there is plenty of time!' 'Ah!' said the chief of devils, 'Go, and you will ruin people by the thousand.'

Though it is only a fable the message is very clear and true. To think that we have plenty of time usually leads to disaster. There is a word which means that we shouldn't put off until tomorrow an important task which could well be done today. It is **Procrastination**. You may well have heard the saying 'Procrastination is the thief of time'.

How much better it would be to get down to homework as soon as you get home or immediately after your meal, so that you will know exactly how much time you have left for your other interests; and those simple tasks which your parents ask you to do, why not do them straight away and get them over with? 'Strike while the iron is hot' is a proverb offering good advice. The blacksmith, when the iron has become red hot, must strike it straight away in order to bend it to the right shape. Should he delay and allow the metal to cool he will have missed his chance. Grasp each new opportunity as it arises.

Christian application

Jesus knew full well the value of time and the danger of procrastination. That is why he said, 'I must work the works of him that sent me while it is day, the night comes when no man can work'.

It would be sad to say that we will only consider following Jesus when we get older. Now is the best time to start. How much we would miss if we were to delay such an important decision.

Reading John 9, 1–5 (For additional research see also 2 Corinthians 6, 2, and Hebrews 3, 8.)

Prayer No 8

Hymn 'Just as I am, your child to be' (for younger children)
'O Jesus I have promised'

Ps and Qs

Week 4

Aim To encourage a respectful attitude towards others
Visual Aid A card with the letters **p** and **q** as shown, and cards with the French words **queue** and **pieds**

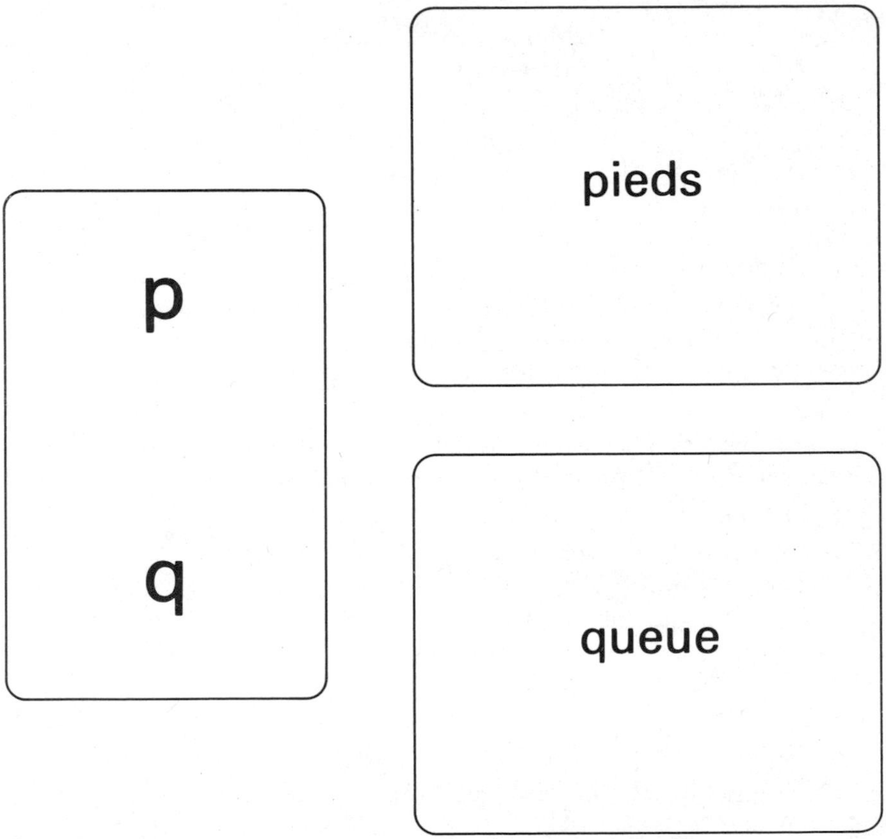

Julie had just been rude to her father. She had dared to answer him back. Quite rightly her dad wasn't going to tolerate this and said, 'Now then, any more of that and I will have to stop your pocket money. It's about time you learned to watch your Ps and Qs.'

Of course we all know that we should speak and behave in a

polite, courteous way towards others. This is often called 'Minding our Ps and Qs'. What a strange expression! How did it originate? Here are three possible explanations:

First explanation: The expression originated in the seventeenth century, when young men attended classes to learn how to dance. The fashion of the time decreed that they should also wear a wig with a pony tail – this in French was called a *queue*. During a vigorous dance this could swish round and catch other dancers. If the young student of dancing was not very proficient he might also step on someone else's feet. The French for feet is *pieds*. He would frequently be told by his teacher to mind his *pieds* and *queues*.

Second explanation: The expression originated in taverns or alehouses where a regular customer could buy his beer on credit. Instead of paying for it there and then, the landlord would chalk it up on a slate and indicate whether the customer had had a pint or a quart (2 pints) of beer, by putting a 'p' or a 'q' against his name. Unscrupulous landlords waited until their clients had had too much to drink and then, hoping that it would not be noticed would put a 'q' instead of a 'p'. If the drinker was still sober enough he might remind the landlord to watch his Ps and Qs.

Third explanation: The third theory goes back to the early days of printing. When the letters were being set up they had to be fixed in a block. As all the letters were back to front it was easy to confuse the P and Q.

Whatever the real origins may be, the meaning is the same for us. We must always show a respectful attitude to others, to our friends, teachers and parents.

Christian application

There is no better advice than that which Jesus gives, that we should treat others as we would wish them to treat us.

Reading	Matthew 7, 7–12
Prayer	No 9 or No 10
Hymn	'For I'm building a people of power'

Worms

Week 5

Aim	To show how we can be of use to others
Visual Aid	A tin box with lid. A card with the words **Antropus pulsatoria** and **Lampyris**

You wouldn't dream of calling each other names would you? No one likes being called names. You wouldn't be at all pleased if someone called you a horrible slimy worm!

Today I am telling you to be like worms.

What do you think is in this tin box? (*Take the lid off slowly.*) That's very strange – they were in the box when I put it here on the table earlier. I wonder where they have got to.

Oh, I remember now, I must have forgotten to put them in in the first place.

I wonder why you were so alarmed at the thought of worms escaping. Are they so objectionable? Why, then, do I want you to be like worms – three particular types of worm?

1 Earthworms. Have you realised how much we need earthworms? They wriggle about in the soil, for the most part without being noticed. They break up the soil so that the air can get to it. Every gardener or farmer understands the importance of earthworms. Without them we would not be able to grow our plants or crops. What a tremendous amount of good they do without being seen.

Be like earthworms! Without having to be seen all the time, just go about your business quietly doing good and being helpful.

2 Bookworms. Yes, there really is such a thing as a bookworm. Its correct name is *Atropus pulsatoria*. It is the tiny larva of a moth or beetle which feeds on paper or the glue used in books.

A person who spends a lot of time reading and loves to study books is often nicknamed a bookworm. We can all learn a great deal from reading books. Make use of the school or public libraries where you will find so many exciting books to read. What a pleasant change this will make, instead of being glued to the television. Try to be more of a bookworm.

3 Glow-worm. This is really a female beetle called *Lampyris* which gives out light from under its abdomen. The purpose of this is to attract other beetles. When it comes to giving out light we should be shining examples to others.

You will now see why I said I want you to be like worms: earthworms, bookworms and glow-worms.

Christian application

The theme of our assembly today is particularly relevant to the Christian gospel, for Jesus told his disciples to go about quietly doing good.

1st Reading Matthew 6, 1–4.

When Paul wrote his second letter to Timothy, he advised him to study God's word so that he would be better equipped to do God's work (see 2 Timothy 2, 15). In his letter to the Ephesians, Paul says that the word of God is an essential part of the Christian's protection against evil.

2nd Reading Ephesians 6, 14–18

And Jesus himself tells us to be shining examples to others.

3rd Reading Matthew 5, 13–16

Prayer No 9

Hymn 'Ye servants of God'

'Fill thou my life O Lord my God'

The strongest man *Week 6*

Aim To show where true strength lies

Visual Aid *The Guinness Book of Records*

Who was the world's strongest man? This is a very difficult question to answer, but if we turn to reference books such as the *Guinness Book of Records* we are given useful information.

For example, could the strongest man have been Paddy Doyle? You may well say that you have never heard of him, but his claim to fame is that in 1988/9 he achieved a documented 1,500,230 press-ups in one year, an all-time world record. That surely required strength.

What about the achievement of Don Ritchie from Great Britain? What did he do? He held the official record for the fastest run from John O'Groats to Lands End, covering the distance in 10 days, 15 hours and 27 minutes. This was another great test of stamina.

(*Note*: These records taken from *The Guinness Book of Records* are revised each year.)

These are all different types of strength. I believe the greatest strength you can have is strength of character. By this I mean the strength to say 'NO' when others tempt you to do something you know is wrong; that is the power to resist temptation.

Christian application

The strongest man of the Old Testament you will recall is Samson who was so strong that he was able to break new ropes like thread (Judges 16, 12). Alas, he allowed himself to be tempted by Delilah, forsaking vows he had made to God.

When the Philistines took him and bound him he thought his great strength could be used to overcome them but he did not know that the Lord had left him. This amazing story can be found in the book of Judges and makes compelling reading.

Samson's strength was God-given. When we turn to the New Testament we are told that Jesus will give his followers the strength they need to overcome trials, tribulations, temptations. In this sense, the strongest people are those who know that the Lord is with them and will give them his strength.

Reading Philippians 4, 8–13. Paul said that we can do all the things God wants us to do if we rely upon Jesus to give us strength.

Prayer No 11

Hymn 'Soldiers of Christ arise' (note the line 'strong in the strength which God supplies')

Ichthus

Week 7

Theme Having the courage of our convictions
An assembly for Whitsuntide

Visual Aid A card with a symbolic diagram of a fish:

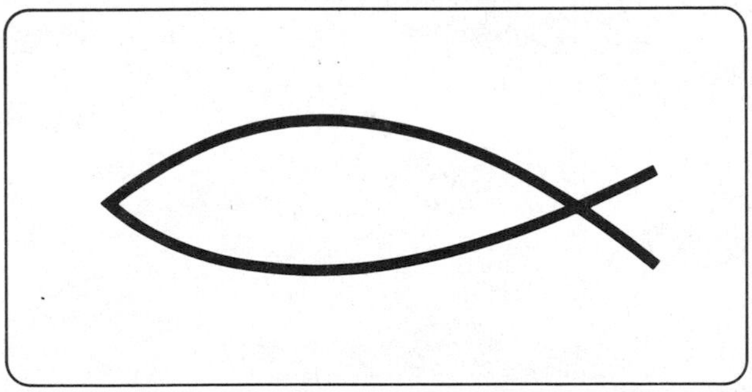

A card with the words:

Ι Χ Θ Υ Σ

I C H T H U S

Lisa was trying to get into her classroom. She was beating on the door and shouting, 'Open the door, let me in!'. Those on the inside were preventing her from doing so and said, 'You can't come in unless you give the password and show the secret sign'. 'How can I when I don't even know it?' replied Lisa. 'In that case you will have to stay outside, this is a secret club,' was the reply.

None of us like it when others seem to have secrets and are not willing to let us know what is going on. It was a bit like that in the early Christian church. The members had a secret sign – the sign of the fish – which was a good way for them to identify one another at a time when they were in danger of being thrown to the lions. The sign they used was very appropriate. These Greek letters spell the word for fish – which is pronounced *Ichthus* – but in Greek the letters also make the beginning of the words **Jesus Christ God's Son Saviour**.

Even today it is necessary in some parts of the world for Christians to worship in secret. How fortunate we are to live in a country where there is freedom of speech and freedom to worship.

Shortly after the events of the first Easter the disciples of Jesus had shut themselves away from the world in a secret upper room. They were afraid to venture outside lest they themselves should also be taken prisoner and crucified like their Master. Although they believed, they did not have the courage of their convictions. Then an amazing thing happened.

Reading Acts 2, 1–8

The followers of Jesus were given the courage and the power they needed to go out into the market place and tell others about the wonderful love of the Lord Jesus. They had received God's power, the Holy Spirit. No longer is the Christian church like a secret club. Everyone is welcome to join. Like the early disciples, we too can be given the courage of our convictions.

Prayer	No 6 or No 33
Hymn	'Stand up, stand up for Jesus' 'For I'm building a people of power'

The Vicar of Bray

Week 8

Aim	To show the need for reliability
Audio Aid	The pianist could be asked to play the tune to the ballad 'The Vicar of Bray'

There is a delightful village called Bray in the county of Berkshire, which is famous for having a vicar, in the sixteenth century, who kept changing his allegiance, whenever there was a change of monarch in the land. He was so renowned that the Oxford Dictionary defines the Vicar of Bray as a 'systematic turncoat'. Legend has it that the Vicar of Bray was first a Roman Catholic but then became a Protestant. He then returned to the Roman Catholic faith but finally became a Protestant again.

Here, first of all, is the tune for the famous ballad which was written about the Vicar of Bray.

Now listen to the words of the ballad and see if you can spot the times when the vicar changed his beliefs to suit the reigning monarch of the day.

The Vicar of Bray
(author unknown)

In good King Charles' golden days,
When loyalty no harm meant,
A zealous High Churchman was I
and so I got preferment.
To teach my flock I never missed,
Kings were by God appointed,
And damn'd are those that do resist
Or touch the Lord's anointed.
For this law I will maintain
Until my dying day, sir,
Whatever King in England reign
I'll be the Vicar of Bray, sir.

When Royal James obtained the crown,
and Popery came in fashion,
The penal laws I hooted down
and read the Declaration,

The Church of Rome I found would fit
Full well my constitution,
And had become a Jesuit
But for the revolution.

When William was our King declar'd
To ease a nation's grievance,
With this new wind about I steer'd,
and swore to him allegiance.
Old principles I did revoke
Set conscience at a distance,
Passive obedience was a joke,
A jest was non-resistance.

When gracious Anne became our Queen,
The Church of England's glory,
Another face of things was seen,
And I became a Tory.
Occasional conformist's case
I damn'd their moderation,
And thought the Church in danger was
By such prevarication.

When George in Pudding-time came o'er
And moderate men looked big Sir,
I turned a cat-in-a-pan once more,
And so I became a Whig Sir.
And thus preferment, I procured
From our new faith's defender,
And almost every day abjured
The Pope and the Pretender.

The illustrious House of Hanover
And Protestant succession,
To these I do allegiance swear
While they keep possession.
For in my faith and loyalty
I never more will falter,
And George my lawful King shall be
Until the times shall alter.

Repeat chorus after each verse.

An important lesson to be learned is how, on the one hand, to listen to the opinions of others and modify our own if necessary, yet on the other hand have the courage to remain true to our convictions.

Christian application
Reliability is just one of the qualities Jesus would like to see in his disciples. He must have been very sad when Peter denied that he was one of his followers. The reading is an account of what happened when Jesus had been taken prisoner and had been led away to be tried.

Reading Matthew 26, 69–75

But Peter was given another chance and became a leader in the early church, showing that he had learned the need to be reliable.

Prayer No 8

Hymn 'Who is on the Lord's side?'
'Be bold, be strong'

The ant

Week 9

Aim To show that we each have a part to play

Preparatory note: Aesop was probably a slave who lived in Greece 2,500 years ago. Tradition has it that though he was ugly and deformed he was very clever. The wise stories he told, fables, made him very famous. Here is one of Aesop's fables:

The ant and the dove
One hot summer day an ant went to the river for a drink of water. But he fell into the river and could not get out. From a nearby tree a dove saw that the ant was in danger and decided to help. So the dove picked up a leaf and dropped it into the water near the ant. 'Climb on to the leaf', said the dove, 'And you will get safely to the bank'.

The ant did as he was told and was so grateful that he promised to help the dove one day.

Not long after, a man came along with a bow and arrow to do some hunting. Seeing the dove on a branch of the tree he took careful aim. Just in time, the ant spotted that the dove was in grave danger so he bit the man on the leg just as he was about to release the arrow, causing it to fly harmlessly up into the air.

As the dove flew to safety she said to the ant, 'Thank you! You did help me after all'.

Aesop said the moral of his story is that no one is too little to be helpful.

Never think you are too small, too insignificant, too unimportant to be of help. We each have an important contribution to make to the life of the school.

Christian application
Similarly in the Lord's service. Though we may not be leaders or have a prominent part to play like the prophets of old, we have all been given some talents to use in his service. 'Don't hide your light', said Jesus. Neither must we hide or bury our talent like the man in this story.

Reading Matthew 25, 14–29. The parable of the talents.
Prayer No 24
Hymn 'God entrusts to all, talents few or many'
'Jubilate ev'rybody'

Talents
by B J Wilcock

I have no particular gifts,
Talents have I none,
Why ask me to help at all?
You carry on!

But God gives gifts to each of us
Whether old or young,
Talents, free, to use each day,
Our whole life long.

Some have many, some have few,
Numbers matter not,
What of those he gave to you?
Waste them not!

When our days on earth are ended
God will want to know,
Have we used the talents given us
Long ago?

Through

Week 10

Aim To encourage an appreciation of how much we owe to others
Visual Aid The sign for No-Through Road

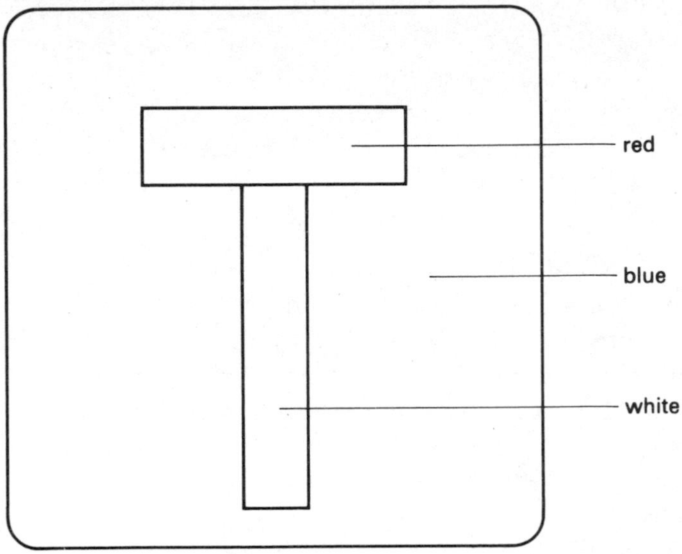

I want you to see if you can spot the connection between the stories I am going to relate.

Story 1: Jason and William had been fighting again. This particular quarrel had been coming to the boil for a few days. When it developed into a fight the dinner lady had no choice. She had to send them to the head teacher. Having considered all the facts the head teacher told them to apologise to the dinner lady for causing her inconvenience, and then gave them a suitable reprimand. As they were leaving Jason said to William, 'It was all through you! You shouldn't have taken my pen in the first place.'

Story 2: Helen badly wanted to join the local dramatic society. But the standards were very high and anyone who wished to join had to have an audition, a sort of test to see whether they could act. She was very nervous when she went out on Saturday afternoon for her audition. Mum and Dad were wondering whether she would pass or not and held their breath when Helen returned before tea-time. 'Now, how did you get on?' they said. Helen announced with a note of triumph. 'I got through!'

Story 3: Jonathan didn't really like singing. He had only joined the school choir because his friends had persuaded him that it was great. But Jonathan preferred to be doing something else. When his friends said, 'Come on Jonathan it's time to go to the choir practice,' he replied, 'I'm not coming, I'm fed up, I'm through with it!'

Story 4: The family was travelling by car to their holiday destination. It was a long way and they were all very tired, including Dad who had been doing all the driving. However, they reached the outskirts of the resort where they were to stay and Dad turned left along a narrow road and drove slowly, looking for the guest house. 'That's funny,' said Dad, 'This road has come to an abrupt end – there's no way out!' 'Didn't you see the sign when you entered the road?' said Susan. (*Show the No-Through Road sign*.) 'This is a no-through road!'

Now, what was the connection? They all contain different uses of the word 'through'. It was *through* William that Jason got into trouble. Helen got *through* her audition for the play. Jonathan was *through* with the choir. Dad drove up a 'No *through* road'.

You must persevere in order to get *through* your problems.

If you do your best, you stand a good chance of getting *through* your exams.

Are others helped and encouraged *through* the example we set?

If you listen to people who tell you there is no need to work hard, you could find yourself travelling along a no-*through* road.

We owe a great deal to many different people. It is through their help that we have been successful.

Christian application

The one to whom we owe the most is the Lord Jesus Christ for 'We have peace with God through our Lord Jesus Christ' (Romans 5, 1); 'The gift of God is eternal life through Jesus Christ' (Romans 6, 23); 'We give glory to God through Jesus Christ' (Romans 16, 27).

Reading	Romans 5, 1–5
Prayer	No 15 or No 16 or No 18
Hymn	'Through all the changing scenes of life'

Greetings cards

Week 11

Aim	To show that life has its ups and downs
Visual Aids	A selection of greetings cards – displayed

You see before you today quite an array of greetings cards. Let's have a look at them in turn.

1 Arrival of baby – always a time for rejoicing.

2 Birthday – we all like to receive cards on our special day.
3 Congratulations on passing your exams – I hope you will all qualify to receive a card like this one day.
4 Valentine's Day card – would you be embarrassed or pleased to receive one?
5 18th Birthday } When will you choose to have your coming of age?
6 21st Birthday } It used to be 21, now the official age is 18.
7 Congratulations on passing your driving test.
8 Engagement congratulations – and then in due course . . .
9 Wedding congratulations.
10 Bon Voyage – I wonder if any of you will choose to live abroad. This card wishes a safe journey to those going abroad.
11 Welcome to your new home.
12 Mother's Day } It is right and proper to honour our parents.
13 Father's Day }
14 Get Well – Most people at some time in their lives have to contend with sickness or accident. It helps at such times to have the good wishes of friends.
15 Christmas cards – the greatest number of Christmas cards sent out by one person was 62,824 by a Mrs Erhard of San Francisco in 1975.
16 Easter cards – are not as common as Christmas cards, though Easter is, perhaps, even more important.
17 Retirement – the thought hasn't even entered your head! But there may be some on the staff who are looking forward to having a well-earned rest and the opportunity of pursuing new interests.
18 Sympathy – it is good to send greetings to our friends on special days. The cards we have seen today mark some special event in our lives. It is a fact of life, however, that one day it will come to an end. This is a sad time for the relatives of the deceased, but it is a great comfort to receive the sympathetic thoughts of loved ones at such a time.

(*Mention here could be made of an expression of sympathy currently being sent on behalf of the school.*)

Christian application

All the cards we have considered convey some greeting or other. How marvellous it would be if one day we received the Lord's special greeting, 'Well done thou good and faithful servant'.

Reading	Psalm 23
Prayer	No 7, No 56, No 38 or No 36, depending on circumstances
Hymn	'The King of love my shepherd is' 'One more step along the world I go'

Stones

Week 12

Aim	To show that everyone can make an important contribution An end-of-year assembly
Visual Aid	Some gemstones. Cards with the words **milestone**, **millstone**, **gemstone**, **cornerstone**

Today's assembly is all about stones.

Milestones were erected by the Romans to indicate to travellers how far they had travelled and the distance to the next destination. A mile represented 1,000 paces by a Roman soldier. Accurately it measures 1,760 yards or 1.60934 metres. The word 'milestone' is also applied to any stage or reckoning point in a person's life or career. Today you have reached another milestone, for you have completed another year in your school career.

Millstones are large, round, flat stones which were used in olden days at mills for grinding corn. You may still see these stones propped up in old farm yards.

Jesus felt so strongly that people should not harm little children that he said that it would even be better for such a person to have a millstone hung around his or her neck and be thrown into the sea.

People now refer to any handicap or burden as a millstone. You have reached a milestone and for the vast majority the year has been very successful but, alas, for just a few who have not paid attention in lessons or have not done homework thoroughly, these shortcomings have been like millstones for them, weighing them down.

Gemstones such as these are precious stones but the term applies also to anyone who is valuable. I am pleased to report that during the year you have made a valuable contribution to the life of the school. You have been real *gems*. Many of you have taken on responsible tasks and have become leaders, monitors, prefects, captains, etc., which brings us to our next stone . . .

Cornerstones are the stones at the corners of buildings and are of great importance, for they hold together the walls of a building. Some of you have, during the year, been like cornerstones. (*Mention could be made of some and appropriate thanks given.*)

Christian application
As we now look to the future we put our trust in Jesus Christ who should be the chief cornerstone of our lives.

Readings	Psalm 118, 21–25 and Ephesians 2, 19–22. Christ the cornerstone.
Prayers	No 49 and No 50
Hymn	'Forth in thy name O Lord I go' 'One more step along the world I go'

Supplement

1 Hide and seek

Aim To show how we can find Jesus as our friend

Visual Aid 1 Either a poster with a series of black shapes, as illustrated below

or

Black shapes cut out to be attached, in order, to a lighter coloured background

2 A Word Search book

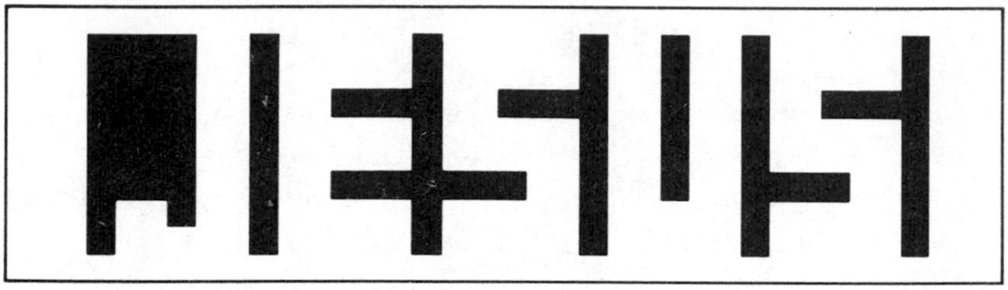

Five, ten, fifteen, twenty, twenty-five, thirty, thirty-five . . . coming ready or not! You will no doubt recall playing the game of Hide-and-Seek when you were much younger. There are, of course, many variations of the popular children's game. Even the army, when engaged in manoeuvres, pursue a similar activity as tanks or reconnaissance or spotter planes search out 'enemy' positions.

Much of your time at school will be taken up searching for knowledge or seeking to find out the answers to various problems. Our work becomes much more interesting if we look upon it as an exciting challenge to find solutions to puzzles. You all enjoy word searches like these (*show book*).

Here is a different puzzle for you to think about today. Look at these black shapes. What do you see? Is there anything hidden? Put up your hand as soon as you 'find' the hidden name. (*Pause.*) It may help if you concentrate less on the shapes and more on the background. (*After a suitable time has elapsed, point out the name* Jesus.)

That was an interesting experiment wasn't it? What can we learn from it?

1 The black shapes remained a puzzle until we saw the name – Jesus – appear. Even our lives can be a puzzle but when we put our trust in Jesus, he is able to make our lives more meaningful.
2 Some pupils didn't at first see Jesus because they were

concentrating on the wrong shape. How much better it is to look at the pleasant things in life, the good things in the world rather than thinking all the time about the bad or even wicked things which go on. It is better, said Paul, to 'Look to Jesus, the author and finisher of our faith' (Hebrews 12, 2).

3 Whenever this puzzle is shown to people it takes some much longer than others to see Jesus. This, too, may be true of the response we make to God's love. There are people who do not respond at all and some who take longer than others. How much we miss if we delay. How much better to do as the Bible says, 'Remember the Creator in the days of your youth' (Ecclesiastes 12, 1). Our lives would become so much more meaningful, we would have the assurance that God is a loving and forgiving Father and we would find that he is longing to help us and direct our paths (Proverbs 3, 5 and 6).

There is a saying, 'Procrastination is the thief of time'. It means that we shouldn't put off until tomorrow what we can well do today. We can all find Jesus today by putting our trust in him and in our prayers ask him to be with us in all we do (see John 1, 12, John 6, 37, Matthew 11, 28, Revelation 3, 20).

4 Now that you have seen the word Jesus on this card, you should be able to see it straight away every time you look at it. This reminds us of the Lord's promise that once we have found him, he will always be with us. He said, 'Lo! I am with you always, to the end of the age'.

Reading Luke 11, 1–10
Prayer No 15
Chorus 'Ask and it shall be given unto you'

2 Volcanoes

Aim To illustrate the desirability of self-control
Visual Aid A diagram of a volcano

The theme of our assembly today is volcanoes. Did you know that between twenty and thirty volcanoes erupt each year? Fortunately the majority of these don't cause any damage.

Volcanoes can simply be long cracks in the ground or can be cone-shaped mountains. The diagram shows what happens when a volcano erupts. Gas and hot molten rock surge through the crack in the

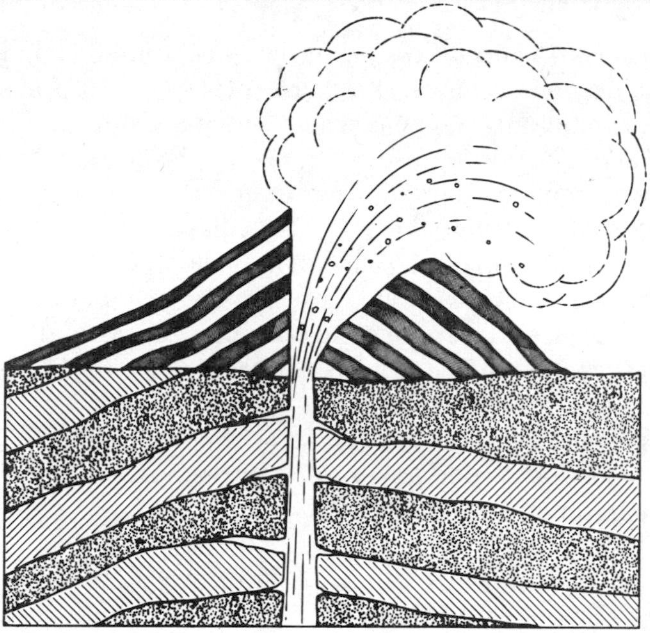

Cone-shaped volcano

earth's crust. The poisonous gas can kill human beings and wildlife over a large area, whilst the molten rock, called lava, can cover whole towns. Because some volcanoes can be very violent, the lives of people living near a live volcano can be at risk. They do well to take note of tell-tale earthquakes caused by liquid rock inside the earth splitting rocks apart as it works its way to the surface, since this could be a warning that a volcano which has been dormant for many years is about to erupt.

Here is some information for you about famous eruptions!

Mount Vesuvius, in Italy, erupted in AD 79, throwing thick layers of ash down on to the nearby city of Pompeii, completely burying it. This ash preserved the buildings and contents for centuries until the site was discovered and excavations began in 1763.
Nevado del Ruiz, a volcano in Colombia, erupted in 1985 and in so doing started a disastrous mud flow which covered a nearby town with a layer of ash and rock, killing 20,000 people.
Stromboli, a volcano off the Italian coast, erupts every twenty minutes.
Mauna Loa, situated in Hawaii, is the largest live volcano. One of its eruptions lasted for one and a half years.

The most dangerous thing about volcanoes is that no one can ever be really sure when they are next going to erupt.

Some pupils I know, and some grown-ups too, have tempers which are like volcanoes. They may behave perfectly well for a period of time, then something happens which provokes an eruption and their temper flares up causing distress to those who happen to be nearby. Some have tempers which are unpredictable, whilst others are like Stromboli and feel that they regularly have to 'blow their top'.

How much more pleasant our school would be if everyone learned to control their tempers. If ever you are provoked and you feel your blood rising, just pause, count to ten and ask yourself if any good would be accomplished by losing your temper.

Christian application
The Bible has some good advice to offer to those who are tempted to lose their temper:

Reading Proverbs 15, 1–5. 'A soft answer turns away wrath.'

Always remember it takes two to make an argument. Remember that Jesus himself said, 'Everyone who is angry with his brother is liable to judgement'.

Prayer No 9
Hymn 'Dear Lord and Father of mankind'

3 Ties

Aim To show that some faults need drastic remedies
Visual Aid An old tie, worn by presenter or alternatively a boy could be asked to wear an old school tie from lost property

Introduction A: Would you believe it, I have put on the wrong tie this morning. This one doesn't really go with this shirt, and just look at the bottom, it is frayed. I know what I had better do (*Take a pair of sharp scissors, cut off two inches, then re-shape it*). Oh! look at that, I've just noticed there is a dirty mark part way up. I'll have to do something about that as well! (*Cut off remaining tie just below the knot.*)

Introduction B: Jason, will you just come here a moment? Is that the best school tie you've got? It doesn't look very smart to me. What has happened to the bottom, it's frayed. (*Take pair of scissors, cut off a couple of inches and re-shape.*) And just look at that dirty mark. We'll have to do something about that. (*Again cut off the tie, this time near the top.*)

That may have shocked some of you. I'd like to thank Jason for his help. He knew what was happening. Here, you may have your own tie back.

It would have been better to remove the offending tie and replace it with a more suitable one.

Some people try to treat bad habits in a light-hearted way. They think they are not very serious and prefer to overlook them. It is much better to get rid of them completely and start afresh. (*At this point the presenter could mention any current bad habits, for example, lateness for lessons, dropping litter, etc.*)

Christian application
In the Bible God doesn't mince words. He calls bad habits sins, and warns that they can separate us from God (see Isaiah 59, 1 and 2). The good news is that Jesus tells his followers that they can become new creatures (see 2 Corinthians 5, 17 and John 3, 3). Don't snip away at bad habits, ask Jesus to help. After all, that is why Jesus came into the world in the first place.

Reading	John 1, 1–13
Prayer	No 25
Chorus	'Search me O God'
	or
Hymn	'Dear Lord and Father of mankind'

4 Heroes

Aim	To extol the virtue of unsung heroes and heroines
Note	This is a suitable theme for a special festival service. Pupils could be rehearsed to read or recite the various parts or could be encouraged to research additional material.
Visual Aids	Cards with the names of the various heroes or heroines

PRESENTER: In every age there have been people who have been proclaimed by the public to be heroines or heroes. These people have accomplished some outstanding feat in sport or exploration or have made some startling discovery which has benefitted mankind, or they have devoted all their energies to serving others. In our assembly today we will consider some heroines and heroes of the twentieth century.

1ST PUPIL: **Bobby Charlton**. If we made a survey of people you consider to be heroic, the majority would probably be sports personalities. The name Bobby Charlton has become synonymous with fair play and he is acclaimed the world over because of his sportsmanship. He is rightly deemed a hero for his 49 goals scored for England in 106 appearances and was deservedly the Footballer of the Year in 1966, when England won the world cup; he was then European Player of the Year in 1967.

2ND PUPIL: **Ian Botham**. Cricket has not been without its share of heroes, men who have performed remarkably with either bat or ball or in the field. Ian Botham will be remembered for his astonishing accomplishments in all three departments. Not only could he bat with tremendous power but he also became, at one stage, the world's leading wicket-taker in test cricket. Add to this the fact that he is very near the top of the list of the world's best catchers and you see why cricket lovers acclaim him as a hero.

The 1987 test series against Australia was probably the highlight of his career. The third test match at Headingly was one of the most sensational ever played. England were already one down in the series and needed to win this match. By mid-afternoon on the fourth day many England players had abandoned hope and had even checked out of their hotel. England still needed 92 runs to avoid an innings defeat with only three wickets left; an impossible task, so everyone thought – except Ian Botham. He destroyed the Australian bowling as he rushed to 145 not out, giving England a lead of just 129 runs which, as it turned out, was just enough for them to win the match. This fine innings inspired the team to go on to win the next two matches and the series.

3RD PUPIL: **Virginia Wade**. It was a great thrill for the British people in 1977 when Virginia Wade won the Ladies Wimbledon Championship, appropriately in the year of the Silver Jubilee of Queen Elizabeth II. This accomplishment alone made Virginia a heroine, but we must not overlook the contribution she made to British tennis from 1965 to 1985. During this time she played in a record 21 ties of the Wightman Cup, a competition between Great

Britain and the United States of America. She also played a record 100 matches in the Federation Cup, that is, the international team championship.

4TH PUPIL: **Captain Scott**. You will all have heard of Captain Scott, the British Antarctic explorer whose deeds were so heroic that he is now commonly known as Scott of the Antarctic. On 18th January, 1912, he got to the South Pole only to discover that the Norwegian explorer, Amundsen, had narrowly beaten him to it and had become the first person to reach it. On the return journey, Captain Scott and his companions, Wilson, Oates, Bowers and Evans all died but not long afterwards Scott's journal was recovered and it was published in 1913.

5TH PUPIL: **Alcock and Brown**. In these days, when air travel is commonplace, it is difficult to realise that it was only in 1919 that the first non-stop flight across the Atlantic was made by John William Alcock and Lieutenant Whitten Brown in a Vickers Vinny biplane. These were exciting times when daring feats of aviation caught the public eye and aviators became heroes.

6TH PUPIL: **Amy Johnson**. Not all aviators were men. One of the most famous and heroic was Amy Johnson who in 1930 set off in her £600 second-hand Gypsy Moth plane on a 10,000-mile solo flight to Australia. She came close to death several times during the nineteen-day flight and was almost hurled into a shark-filled sea near Singapore. At the age of 27 she was awarded the CBE by King George V for her astonishing bravery.

7TH PUPIL: **Albert Schweitzer**. This man could have made a fortune as an organist or as a surgeon or as a writer. Indeed he was awarded the Nobel Peace Prize in 1952 for one of his exhortations. But instead he devoted his life to work as a missionary and in this work he founded a hospital, such was his concern for other people. He only gave organ recitals to raise money to help the work in his hospital. He was a real hero.

8TH PUPIL: **Mother Teresa**. What a truly remarkable person. Mother Teresa's name will always be revered the world over for her unstinting love and compassion for the sick and needy, the dying and especially for children who have been abandoned. For her Christian work Mother Teresa was also awarded the Nobel Peace Prize in 1979 and an honorary Order of Merit in 1983.

PRESENTER: The famous people we have considered in our assembly are just a selected few of the many who have thrilled others by their exploits and who we think of as heroes.

But for everyone who has been brought to the forefront of the public's attention there are countless thousands whose deeds go unnoticed or who do not receive public acclaim. These are the unsung heroes, people who quietly go about their business serving the community and showing compassion and concern for the less fortunate.

In our school there are those who rightly receive recognition: the captains of the various sports teams, the leading scorers, those who excel in examinations, those who take on the responsibilities of leadership. The success of our school or any community depends just as much upon the vast majority of unsung heroes who, each in their quiet way, make an invaluable contribution to our lives.

Christian application

For us to go about our business quietly is what God's word teaches us. This is what Jesus said in the Sermon on the Mount:

Reading Matthew 6, 1–6

The Bible tells us of the person who must surely be the greatest hero of all, Jesus himself. Knowing what would befall him in Jerusalem (that he would be taken captive, tried and then crucified) Jesus set his face steadfastly to go to that city. This was the most amazing act of heroism. Jesus knew that he had to do his heavenly Father's will and that he had to die that we might be forgiven.

'For God so loved the world that He gave His only begotten Son that whosoever believeth in Him should not perish but have everlasting life' (John 3, 16).

Prayer No 8

Hymn 'Who would true valour see'
'For all the saints who from their labours rest'

5 Medals

Aim To show that, though we may not always get medals for our good behaviour, it does pay to be honest, it does give great satisfaction to feel that we have been of help to others

Visual Aid Poster or diagrams of medals as shown

or

Arrange beforehand for selected pupils to bring in

medals which they or members of their family have been awarded.

The Victoria Cross

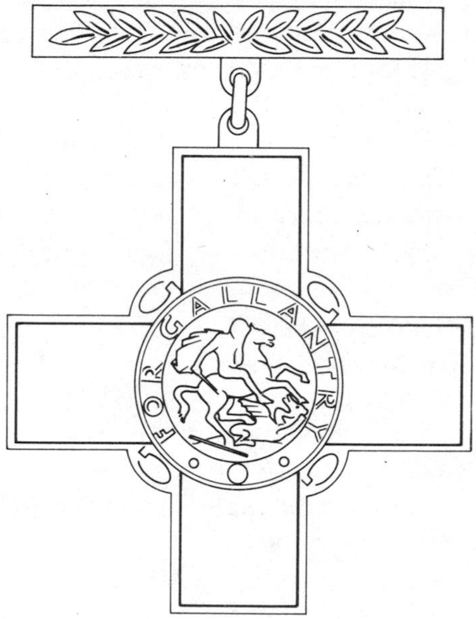

The George Cross

Story 1: Susan's grandmother was very ill and it meant that her parents, who both went out to work, had to rush round to Grandma's every evening to see to her needs. 'Don't bother about the dishes,' Susan said to them, 'I'll do them so that you can get straight off. Give Grandma my love.'

While her parents were away Susan not only washed the tea dishes, she dried them and put them away. She then went round the house with the vacuum cleaner, tidied up and dusted. When her mum and dad returned later and saw the house spick and span they said, 'That is wonderful Susan, you deserve a medal'.

Story 2: James had broken his wrist playing for the school football team. It was his right hand. Most people would have thought there was a small consolation in that he wouldn't be able to do his homework. Indeed, the teacher said, 'I know you won't be able to do this work James, I fully understand.'

But the teacher had a surprise coming, for James showed the same determination as he usually displayed on the football field. He practised writing with his left hand until his writing was just about readable. Though it took him much longer than usual he did manage to complete the exercise. With an apology for the untidiness, he handed in his homework at the appointed time. 'I am impressed with your determination, James, you deserve a medal for trying!'

Have you ever received a medal? Some of our pupils have brought along medals to show you. They will explain why they were awarded. (*At this point any medals brought in by pupils can be shown.*)

I want to tell you next about two of the most famous medals.

The Victoria Cross is given for conspicuous bravery in wartime. It was instituted by Queen Victoria in 1856. Made of bronze the medals are 4cm in diameter and have a crimson ribbon. Until the supply ran out in 1942, they were made from the metal of cannons which had been captured from the Russians at Sevastopol, during the Crimean War. They are now made from gunmetal supplied by the Royal Mint. It would be good to think that no more Victoria Crosses would be awarded, for this would mean that wars were a thing of the past.

The George Cross is the supreme civilian award in Britain for acts of the greatest courage in circumstances of extreme danger. Instituted in 1940, it consists of a silver cross with a medallion in the centre bearing a design of St George and the Dragon.

It is right and proper to give recognition to people for bravery or gallantry. It is right too to give medals for oustanding achievements and service. Many people, like those mentioned in our opening stories, deserved medals but did not receive them. I am sure that everyone here will feel at some time in their lives that they deserve a medal.

I wish I could give a medal to everyone who gets on with the job they have been given, quietly, without fuss and to the best of their ability. I wish, too, that everyone who tries to be helpful to others, everyone who seeks to do what they know to be right, should receive due recognition. Even though these people may be unsung heroes, they do gain something which is invaluable – they have satisfaction.

Christian application

Our reading today tells of the greatest accolade anyone can possibly receive.

Reading Matthew 25, 14–28

We too may receive our Lord's special commendation if we are faithful to him. What a thrill to hear his words, 'Well done, thou good and faithful servant'.

'Blessed is the person who endures temptation, for when they are tried they shall receive the crown of life which the Lord has promised to those who love Him' (James 1, 12).

Prayer No 24
Hymn 'Stand up, stand up for Jesus'

6 They got it wrong

Aim To illustrate the folly of being self-opinionated
Visual Aid A picture of the Leaning Tower of Pisa
Audio Aid A recording of Ravel's 'Bolero'

Poor old Bonanno Pisano got it wrong! He was the architect who in 1174 began to build the famous bell tower for the cathedral of Pisa. By the time the builders reached the fifth floor they discovered that it had developed a severe lean. Bonanno Pisano had miscalculated. He had built his tower on marshy ground with inadequate foundations. Aware of this serious error he fled for his life from Pisa, leaving the completion of the tower to others. At the age of 84 he thought it would be safe to return to Pisa because no one would remember him. But they did! When he eventually died he was buried beneath his famous tower on the side it was leaning towards.

So many people get things wrong and make statements which are, in time, proved to be wrong, for instance:

1 Lord Kelvin was President of the Royal Society from 1890 to 1895 but he couldn't have been more wrong when he said, 'Radio has no future'. He also stated that 'Heavier than air flying machines are impossible'.
2 This is what a professor at Cambridge University said when Frank Whittle showed him his plan for the first jet engine: 'Very interesting, Whittle my boy, but it will never work.'
3 I wonder to what the Mayor of Dover was making reference in 1875 when he said, 'I make bold to say that I don't believe that in the future history of the world any such feat will ever be performed again by anybody else.' Matthew Webb had just become the first person to swim the English Channel.
4 What did the parliamentary committee say in their report when they had been asked to consider Edison's invention of the electric light bulb? They said, 'It is unworthy of the attention of practical or scientific men'.
5 Listen next to what a music critic said in St Petersburg on 13th

November 1875: 'Tchaikovsky's First Piano Concerto, like the first pancake, is a flop!'

6 What about this for a review? 'I would say that this does not belong to the art which I am in the habit of considering music.' That was a review of Beethoven's Fifth Symphony.

7 Now we are going to listen to a short excerpt of a recording of Ravel's 'Bolero', which gained great popularity when Torvill and Dean used it in their world championship ice skating programme.

This is what a music critic said of it in *The American Mercury* in May 1932: 'Ravel's "Bolero" I submit as the most insolent monstrosity ever perpetrated in the history of music.' How wrong he was proved to be.

8 Finally, listen to what was written about Charles Dickens in the *Saturday Review*, 1858: 'We do not believe in the permanence of his reputation; our children will wonder what their ancestors could have meant by putting Dickens at the head of novelists of his day.'

Let's not be too hard on all these people who made mistakes for we *all* from time to time get it wrong. There are two important lessons for us to learn:

- Never be so self-opinionated as to think you know it all – that everyone else is wrong and you are the only one who is right. Always listen to other points of view before you come to a conclusion and before you express an opinion.
- Remember that humility is a great virtue. Realise that everyone makes mistakes and that it often takes courage to admit, 'I got it wrong'. Let us learn by our mistakes.

Christian application

Bonanno Pisano built his tower without sure foundations. Jesus teaches us that people who ignore his teachings get it wrong for they are building upon insecure foundations. But we can get it right when we listen to his words and put our trust in him for then we are building our lives on the best possible foundations.

Reading Matthew 7, 24–28
Prayer No 37
Chorus 'Build on the rock and not upon the sand'
'The wise man built his house upon the rock'
or
Hymn 'Lord of all hopefulness'

7 Golden eggs

Aim To show that greed can be our downfall

Preparatory note: You will all have heard of Aesop and his famous fables. In fact he never wrote down the fables himself, that was left to someone else many years later. He just made up the stories and told them to other people who then passed them on. In time the fables were forgotten, but hundreds of years later in 1844 in the monastery of Mount Athens in Greece they were re-discovered and have since gained world-wide renown, for their moral lessons are as true today as they were when Aesop was alive.

Here is one of his famous stories:

The goose that laid the golden eggs

Once an old man and an old woman had a goose which they discovered could lay eggs which were different from other goose eggs. They were made of solid gold! 'At last we shall be rich,' they said, as each day the goose laid a golden egg. These they sold for lots of money. Alas, the more money they had, the more they wanted and one day they said, 'If the goose lays golden eggs, it must be made of gold itself.' So they cut open the goose hoping to find lots more gold. But they discovered that it was just like any other goose. They had killed the goose which laid the golden eggs.

Aesop said the moral of his story is that a greedy person can lose all he or she has.

Christian application

Jesus told a similar story about the fate of a rich man who wanted more and more.

Reading Luke 12, 16–21. Possessions do not bring real and lasting happiness.

Prayer No 25

Hymn 'Happiness is to know the Saviour'

8 The fox and the stork

Aim To show that we should treat others as we would have them treat us

Visual Aid A flat plate and jug with a long neck

Here is another of Aesop's fables. It is called:
The fox and the stork
One day a fox invited a stork to his house for a meal. The stork agreed to go and thought it was a very nice idea. But he didn't realise that the fox was about to play a trick on him.

When the stork arrived for dinner he found that the fox had put the food on two plates. The fox immediately set about eating his dinner off the plate but, try as he would, the stork was unable to pick up the food from the plate with his long beak. 'What's the matter?' enquired the cunning fox, 'do you not like the meal I have provided? I see I shall have to eat it myself!' So the fox ate both meals.

Soon after, the stork asked the fox to dinner. When the fox arrived he found that the stork had put the food in two jugs with long necks, rather like this one. This time it was the fox who was unable to reach the food and had to stand by while the stork ate both dinners.

Aesop said the moral of his story is that if you play mean tricks on other people, they might do the same to you.

Christian application
Of course two wrongs never make a right and the Bible is much more positive, telling us to do to others as we would have them do to us.

Reading Matthew 5, 38–48
Prayer No 9
Hymn 'When I needed a neighbour'

9 Just my luck!

Aim To show that there is usually someone worse off than we are

Do you ever think to yourself, 'That's just my luck' or 'I must be the unluckiest person in the world'? Next time you are tempted to think like that, just pause for a moment and try to consider the plight of other people who may well be much worse off. I hope you will never have the same experiences as the people I am going to tell you about today!

First, take the case of Mrs Helen Ireland from California, who in the early 1970s failed her driving test in the first second. She got into the car, said, 'Good Morning' to the examiner, and started the engine. However, instead of putting her foot on the clutch she put it on the accelerator and the car shot straight into the wall of the driving test centre.

Then there is the case of the American lady who created a record in 1912 for the worst ever score for a single hole in golf. She took 166 strokes over a short 130-yard hole. Her first shot landed in the river but when, surprisingly, she discovered that the ball floated, she got her husband to take her out in a small rowing boat, on to the river. From the boat she eventually managed to hit the ball on to the river bank two miles down stream. After two hours and 166 strokes she eventually completed the hole.

When it comes to sport, never think that your performance must be the worst ever or that luck is not on your side. Here is an account of the most disastrous cricket match of all time.

At the beginning of the century two schoolboy teams played a match at Cambridge. Trophy Boys XI won the toss and batted first; but they were all out for nought. When King's Choir School went in to bat the first ball was a no-ball, giving away one run. This gave King's Choir a score of one, and victory in the match without any of their players hitting the ball!

These stories were taken from *The Return of Heroic Failures* by Stephen Pile (Secker and Warburg).

Remember that you are not the world's most unlucky person. Disasters don't just happen to you. There are many people in other parts of the world who are far worse off. Let us now think for a few moments of those in . . . . (*Here mention could be made of the sufferings of the victims of some disaster recently making headlines in the news*, eg *those made homeless by floods, or people forced to flee from their homes because of civil war, or those who mourn the loss of loved ones in a terrible air crash, earthquake, etc, or the countless millions dying of starvation in lands where the crops have failed again.*)

When we consider the tragic suffering of these unfortunate people, don't our own problems seem trivial? The peoples of the world who have plenty, who enjoy peace and security must seek ways of helping those who are not as fortunate.

Christian application

In the midst of life's tragedies and sorrows Christians often say that when they turn to God for help he gives them strength and courage to bear their sorrows. Listen now to these words of comfort and reassurance from God's word.

Reading	Psalm 46. God is our refuge and strength; an ever-present help in trouble.
Prayers	No 57 and No 58
Hymn	'He's got the whole world in his hand' 'When I needed a neighbour, were you there?'

10 Hobson's choice

Theme Making the best choices

Tobias Hobson lived at the same time as William Shakespeare and made his living by hiring out horses; rather like rent-a-car. He believed that his horses should take turns to work so that none became over-worked. If a client wanted to hire a horse he would have to take the one which had had the longest rest. This would usually be the one nearest to the stable door. Should a customer prefer the look of one of the other horses, Tobias Hobson would insist on his taking the first one in line, even though they protested vehemently. This became known as 'Hobson's choice': it was a choice between taking the horse which he offered or none at all.

We still use the expression today. Hobson's choice means to have no choice at all. Here are a couple of examples:

There was a particularly good play on at the local theatre and Mr and Mrs Jones were keen to see it. When Mr Jones called at the box office to book seats he was told that there were only two seats left, right at the back. He really wanted better seats but when the attendant said, 'I'm afraid you must either take them or leave them,' he realised that it was a case of Hobson's choice.

When it comes to deciding whether or not to bother coming to school you also have Hobson's choice, for it is the law of the land that you must attend. Similarly it is a school rule that . . . . (homework must be done, uniform must be worn, etc) . . . Another case of Hobson's choice.

If you think carefully about these rules you will appreciate their good sense and realise they are made for your benefit.

In other walks of life we do have a choice to make:

1 You may choose where to go for your family holidays.
2 You have to choose what to wear when you go out for the evening.
3 You may have to choose which new cassette recorder to buy.
4 Here at school you will have to choose which subjects to study.

5 When you are about to leave, you have to choose the career you wish to follow.
6 Later in life you will have to choose where to live.
7 You may wish to choose a life's partner.

In these matters you are free to choose: fortunately you will not be given Hobson's choice.

Christian application
Jesus makes it very clear that we all have a most important choice to make, one which has far-reaching consequences. The choice is between believing in him and not believing. This is like choosing between light and darkness.

Reading	John 3, 17–21
Prayer	No 23
Hymn	'I have decided to follow Jesus'

11 The Persian king

Aim To encourage tolerance of different points of view

A Persian king once wanted to teach his four sons never to jump to hasty conclusions or make rash judgements, so he decided to send them in turn to a part of his country where he knew there was a special mango tree. He sent his eldest son in winter, the next son in spring, the third son in summer and finally the youngest son went in the autumn, all to see the same mango tree. When the last son had returned the king called them all together to describe what they had seen.

'All I saw was a shrivelled-up old stump,' said the eldest son.
'No, you are wrong,' said the second, 'It has a lacy green appearance.'
'I would compare it to a beautiful rose,' said the third son.
'But you are all wrong, it has fruit like a pear,' declared the youngest son.

Before they had chance to begin an argument the king said, 'You all have a different point of view but you are all right because you each saw the mango tree in a different season.'

What a lesson that ancient fable teaches us! We must take time to understand people who hold different opinions from our own, we must get to know them and learn their backgrounds. They may all have important contributions to make. A person who says, 'I'm right in everything I believe and everyone else is entirely wrong,' is called a bigot. Always listen to other people's points of view.

Christian application
This applies to Christians too. We must all listen to the opinions of others, but if we believe we have something to offer which others have not then it is unlikely we will win them over by argument. The best way to convince others that our way is better is by the example of the lives we live. We should be like a good tree which bears good fruit.

Reading	Matthew 7, 17–20
Prayer	No 30 and No 46
Hymn	'Lord speak to me'

12 We haven't heard the last of this!

Aim	To show how the Christian message is relevant for every generation
Theme	A nativity play with a difference

CAST

INNKEEPER
ESTHER – innkeeper's wife
ANDREW – their son
RUTH – a visitor
SIMON – Ruth's husband
TIMOTHY – their son
MARY
JOSEPH
NARRATOR
THREE SHEPHERDS

Carol: 'O little town of Bethlehem'

NARRATOR: The scene is set in a crowded inn in Bethlehem of Judea at the time of the census ordered by Caesar Augustus, the Roman Emperor. The innkeeper is busying himself in the front room when a knocking is heard. He walks across to the door and admits Ruth, Simon and their son, Timothy.

INNKEEPER: Well hello there! How nice it is to meet you again. Let me see, it could be five years since you were here last; and this must be young Timothy. My, how you have grown – quite a young man now! I must say it is a good job you sent word that you were coming otherwise there would have been no room left. As it is I'm afraid the only room available is the small one at the back overlooking the courtyard. All the others have been booked for some time. With this census being carried out everyone seems to be coming to Bethlehem. But there, I mustn't grumble, its good for business and you all look tired. I had better show you to your room.

(*They all leave, but the innkeeper quickly returns.*)

NARRATOR: As the innkeeper returns to his chores he is joined by his wife, Esther. They sit at the table for a brief respite which is interrupted all too soon by Andrew, their son, who appears rather agitated. He stands anxiously waiting to get his parents' attention.

ESTHER: You know, I'm worn to a frazzle, making all those beds. I'm glad its not often that we are fully booked. I suppose it's my own fault! I've known for some time that we were going to be packed out this week-end. I should have planned ahead and got on top of things. Did I see more guests arriving just now? So that's the last room taken!

ANDREW: Dad! Will you come and speak to this chap at the front door? He won't take 'No' for an answer. Says his wife-to-be is expecting a baby, and hasn't got long to go. This census caught him unaware. He has tried all the other accommodation in town, there isn't a room to be had. I told him we were fully booked but he is demanding to see the manager.

(*The innkeeper walks across to the door and begins to speak to someone who is obviously standing outside.*)

INNKEEPER: You heard what my son said, I'm very sorry but there's nothing I can do, every room is now taken. Yes, I appreciate your concern for your wife but I couldn't very well ask someone who has booked weeks ago to give up their room, could I? A shelter and somewhere to sit you say? That's all you want? Well, I hardly like to mention it, but if you are that desperate you could stay the night in the stables. We could move the animals to a separate compartment and we have plenty of clean straw. Of course not, I wouldn't dream of charging you for it. I'm only sorry I haven't anything better to offer.

(*They all leave.*)

NARRATOR: It is now the early hours of the morning and in an upstairs room Ruth is unable to sleep and walks across to the window. She is startled by something and goes over to wake her husband and son.

RUTH: Wake up Simon! Wake up Timothy! Come over here to the window, it's a beautiful night and I want you to see this star. Have you ever seen anything like it? It's certainly the largest and brightest star I have ever seen. You know what they say: a new star heralds the birth of some important person. Yes! that's the one I mean, the one that seems to be directly above the old stable in the courtyard.

(*Pause.*)

Hush! Be quiet a moment. I thought I saw a movement in that far corner of the yard – there you see – are they intruders? There are three of them. I wonder what they are up to. They don't appear to be townsfolk from what I can make out. Look, they are going into the stable.

SIMON: I think we should mention it to the innkeeper first thing in the morning but right now I'm going back to sleep.

(*They all leave.*)

NARRATOR: The three mysterious visitors have departed by the time Ruth, Simon and Timothy come down to report what they had seen to the innkeeper.

INNKEEPER: Thank you for mentioning it, but I was aware of the situation, in fact I feel pretty bad about it. This engaged couple turned up last last night and pleaded for accommodation because the young lady was expecting a baby and was very tired. But I told them we had no room. With hindsight I should have let them have our room. We could always have slept on these benches for one night. It was a bit off expecting them to spend the night in the stable – it's really only fit for animals. To make matters worse the lady did give birth to a son and because there was nowhere else to put him they laid him in an old trough we used to use for the cattle fodder. But what bothers me most is what those men you saw have been telling me. They are shepherds, you know, and have travelled all the way from Galilee, claiming they were told to come here by the angel Gabriel himself and that the child they would find, lying in a manger, would be Christ the Lord. Could it be that God's own son has been born in, of all places, *my* stable? Somehow, I don't think we have heard the last of this.

NARRATOR: How true those words are. *'We certainly have not heard the last of it.'* For two thousand years the good tidings of the birth of God's son have been re-enacted in churches and schools throughout the world at Christmas time.

Tableau: As the players assemble in the inn, the traditional nativity tableau is formed. Joseph escorts Mary who places the baby in the manger. The three shepherds arrive and kneel in adoration.

NARRATOR: And she brought forth her first born son and laid him in a manger because there was no room at the inn. And they called his name Jesus for he shall save his people from their sin.

Prayer No 26
Carol 'It came upon the midnight clear'

(Duration – 10 minutes approximately.)

Note Should a longer presentation be required, the carol 'Away in a manger' could be sung after the tableau has been formed. The three wise men could complete the tableau by making their entrance along the main aisle and singing the first verse and chorus of 'We three kings'.

Prayers

Prayers

1 *A morning prayer*
We thank you dear Father for guarding us during the hours of darkness and for bringing us, renewed and refreshed, to enjoy your gift of a new day. Help us to do our work with diligence, to be patient and considerate toward all whom we meet, and help us to show forgiveness to any who may offend us.

2 *An evening prayer*
At the close of another day, O God, we commit ourselves into your hands. We thank you for your presence during the day which is now past, for your help, guidance and strength. Grant us Lord a restful night that when we awake in the morning we shall be refreshed and renewed for the tasks that lie ahead of us.

3 *For the Bible*
Heavenly Father we praise you and give you thanks for your holy word, the Bible and for the good news contained within its pages. Help us as we read it to see the importance of your word and its relevance for our lives today. May it be a source of strength and a means of guidance as we seek to serve you in the world.

4 *Praise*
O Lord, our God, the whole world is full of your glory, for in the beginning you created the heaven and the earth and you have given us life and the ability to choose between good and evil. Help us, we pray, to love that which is pure and true and to do nothing which would mar your handiwork. May we seek always to do your will.

5 *Gratitude*
We thank you for this new day, heavenly Father, and for the opportunities we shall have of serving you. You have given us so much to make us happy, our homes, health, our friends and our

school. Help us to show our thanks for your love by using all your good gifts aright. Help us, in return for your goodness, to do all we can to make life pleasant for others.

6 *For God's blessing*
Father, may your spirit keep us pure in thought, word and deed, honest in our dealings, kind to one another, and forgiving to any who may offend us. May your blessing be upon our homes, our school, our friends and all whom we love; through Jesus Christ our Lord.

7 *For the sick*
Father in Heaven you know our every need, so this morning we bring to you the needs of . . . . asking that you will be very near to him/her in this time of sickness. Be a source of comfort, encouragement and strength, we pray, and if it is your will, speedily restore him/her to full health and strength.

8 *Use of talents*
O God, our loving Father, we ask you to be with us throughout this day. Help us to do our work well for your sake as for our own. Keep us from idleness and carelessness and help us to use our talents wisely, that nothing may be wasted but that in all things we may be relied upon to do our very best, to love and serve you and our fellow human beings.

9 *Right living*
Heavenly Father we thank you for this new day and its opportunities of serving you. Keep us from anything which might spoil our work or our service. Send your holy spirit upon us, so that we may think pure thoughts, speak clean words and do good deeds. Grant, Lord, that we shall do only that which is right in your sight.

10 *An ancient prayer*
O Lord, our heavenly Father, almighty and everlasting God, who hath safely brought us to the beginning of this day; defend us in the same with thy mighty power, and grant that this day we fall into no sin, neither run into any kind of danger; but that all our

doings, being ordered by thy governance, may be righteous in thy sight; through Jesus Christ our Lord.

11 *A knight's prayer*
My Lord I am ready on the threshold of this new day, to go forth, armed with thy power, seeking adventure on the highroad; to right wrong, to overcome evil, to suffer wounds and endure pain if need be, but in all things to serve thee bravely, faithfully, joyfully, that at the end of the day's labour, kneeling for thy blessing, thou mayest find no blot upon my shield.

12 *An evening prayer*
Lighten our darkness we beseech thee O Lord and by thy great mercy defend us from all perils and dangers of this night, for the sake of thine only son, our Lord and Saviour, Jesus Christ.

13 *Vesper*
Lord keep us safe this night, secure from all our fears, may angels guard us while we sleep, till morning light appears.

14 *Forgiveness*
Loving Father we ask you to forgive us for all the wrong we may have done. Forgive us for the things we should have done and did not do. Help us to be sorry when we do what is not right and help us to try very hard to do better. Thank you, O God, for being a loving and forgiving father. May we, in return, be the sort of people you want us to be.

15 *A prayer of thanksgiving* (After each sentence the pupils make the response, 'We thank you Heavenly Father')
Loving Father, today we give you thanks for all your goodness and for those gifts we often take for granted; for our home and its happiness . . . 'We thank you Heavenly Father'
For our friends and their kindness . . . (Response)
For loving parents and all who care for us . . . (Response)
For our strength and our health . . . (Response)
For times of recreation and times of sleep . . . (Response)
For the interesting things we learn and do . . . (Response)
For Jesus who loves us and died for us . . . (Response)
These our thankful prayers we offer in Jesus' name.

16 *Help*

We thank you heavenly Father for all the good things we enjoy, our health and strength, our homes and our friends. Father we are grateful for all the help given to us by our parents and friends. Help us to be loyal to them and to show by our love and kindness how thankful we are.

17 *Creation*

O God, our heavenly Father, we thank you for our life and health and for every good thing we enjoy. Especially we thank you for making this world such a beautiful place. Help us to remember that it is your world. Forbid, Lord, that we should ever do anything to destroy the environment or mar your handiwork.

18 *For our homes*

O God, our Father in Heaven, we ask today for your blessing upon our homes, our parents, our brothers and sisters and upon all who love and care for us. Help us never to be thoughtless or selfish but always kind to each other. Keep us from quarrelling and from angry words. May we always feel that you are near to us, protecting us, and helping us to live as you would have us live.

19 *A prayer when there has been trouble*

Dear Father we are sorry that we have not helped to make our home/school happy and peaceful. Forgive us, we pray, for those times when we have been selfish, thoughtless, bad-tempered and unkind. Hear us now as we promise to try for better things. (Now we will have a period of silence while we think carefully of ways by which we can bring the love of God into the lives of others.) Help us to keep all these promises for Jesus' sake.

20 *For the sick*

Father in Heaven we know that you have love and compassion for all your children. You know all our needs. We thank you for doctors and nurses and for all who work in hospitals caring for the sick. Be very near, we pray, to all who are ill, especially our friend . . . . . . Help him/her to be patient and grant O Lord that he/she may soon be strong again. We thank you for our own health and strength. May we use these gifts from you to bring help and comfort to those who are less fortunate.

21 *Thanks for harvest*

Almighty God, by whose hand the earth was made, we thank you once again at harvest time for your faithfulness in supplying all our needs especially in providing the food we need. We thank you for farmers, for fishermen and for all who use their skills to bring us your good gifts. Dear God, there are so many in other countries who have insufficient food, indeed many are dying of starvation. Grant Lord that the nations which have plenty may learn to share their riches with those who are less fortunate and so relieve their suffering.

22 *Telling of God's love*

Heavenly Father, help us to see how the world needs your love and healing power. May the good news of the Lord Jesus Christ be told in every land so that men and women, boys and girls may come to know him and the world become a better place where your will is done. Help us to play our own small part in this great task.

23 *Overcoming temptation*

Dear Lord, you know how difficult it is for us, sometimes, to do what is right. Help us always to fight against the wrong. Help us to be brave when we are afraid; to be cheerful when we are disappointed, to be pleasant when we feel angry. Help us always to be truthful even when we mistakenly think it will make matters worse. Lord give us the strength we need to overcome temptation, to make wise decisions and to follow the example which you have set for us, for you are the way, the truth and the life.

24 *For difficult tasks*

Lord you promised to give your disciples the strength they needed in times of difficulty. Help us today to fulfil the tasks you have given us to do. Sometimes our work seems difficult but we thank you that we are only called upon to do our best. May we always seek to use our talents well and to do your will, knowing that you will be with us, giving us the strength we need.

25 *Forgiveness*

Heavenly Father, we are sorry that so often we fall short of the standards you set for us, for we are sometimes selfish, inconsiderate, greedy, unkind and lazy. We thank you that you are a loving and a forgiving father. Give to us all clean hearts we pray and the strength we need to live more like our Lord and Saviour Jesus Christ who gave his life for us.

26 *Christmas prayer*
Heavenly Father we thank you for sending your son Jesus Christ at Christmastime to be our friend and saviour and to reveal your love for us. As we think of his lowly birth in the stable at Bethlehem may we now prepare ourselves to receive him into our lives so that we too may be able to play a small part in bringing joy to others and so make this a season of peace and goodwill.

27 *Thank you for Jesus*
Heavenly Father we thank you for the joyous tidings of Christmas Day, that you so loved the world that you gave us the greatest gift of all, that of your son, Jesus Christ. We thank you that he was once a child like us. Help us to follow his example, to grow wise and strong like him. We thank you that he came to be our Saviour. Help us to give ourselves in his service.

28 *Easter*
Thank you Lord for Easter time, when everything comes to life again. We thank you for warmer sunnier days and that colourful flowers are re-appearing in our gardens. We thank you for the evidence around us of new life as we see lambs in the fields and the birds making their nests. Help us to remember that the important message of Easter time is that Jesus came back to life after wicked people had crucified him. Thank you that Jesus is alive today and can dwell in our hearts and lives by faith.

29 *Prayer for the sick*
Dear Father we pray that you will cheer and heal those who are sick (especially we name before you our friend . . . .). Grant to physicians, surgeons, doctors and nurses, wisdom and skill, sympathy and patience. Bless, we pray, all who work to prevent suffering.

30 *For the persecuted*
We thank you dear Lord that you have granted to us the freedom to worship you, each in our own way. We pray particularly today for all who do not enjoy such freedom but are

instead persecuted for their beliefs. Strengthen them and sustain them O Lord and hasten the day when all people shall glorify your name.

31 *For the elderly*
Dear Lord we pray for all elderly people, especially those known to us who are infirm, lonely or weary. Grant to them strength for their daily needs, grateful memories of the past and assurance of the life which is to come.

32 *For the new day*
We thank you O God for protecting us through the night and for the promise of this new day. As we begin it with you we ask that you will help us to meet all challenges with quiet confidence. Strengthen us against temptation and keep us always loyal to our families, our friends, our school and above all to yourself.

33 *A traditional prayer* (for the Holy Spirit's guidance)
Heavenly Father in whom we live and move and have our being, we humbly pray thee so to guide and govern us by thy Holy Spirit, that in all the cares and occupations of our daily life we may never forget thee, but remember that we are ever walking in thy sight, through Jesus Christ our Lord.

34 *Traditional prayer* (for purity of heart)
Almighty God, unto whom all hearts are open, all desires known, and from whom no secrets are hid, cleanse the thoughts of our hearts by the inspiration of thy Holy Spirit, that we may perfectly love thee, and worthily magnify thy holy name; through Christ our Lord.

35 *For thoughtful speech*
Help us, O Lord, to keep guard over our lips. Save us from words that hurt, from gossip and slander and lies. May we speak only to encourage and cheer and grant that all we say shall be to your praise and glory.

36 *Love towards God* (a traditional prayer)
O God, who has prepared for those who love you such good things as pass our understanding, pour into our hearts such love towards you, that we, loving you above all things, may obtain your promises, which exceed all that we can desire, through Jesus Christ our Lord.

37 *Service* (a traditional prayer)
O thou who art the light of the minds that know thee, the life of the souls that love thee, and the strength of the wills that serve thee; help us so to know thee that we may truly love thee, so to love thee that we may fully serve thee, whom to serve is perfect freedom; through Jesus Christ our Lord.

38 *For those who mourn*
Almighty God who has taught us that those who mourn shall be comforted, grant to the family and friends of .... your peace and consolation. As, in their grief they turn to you, may they experience the assurance of your great love. Through Jesus Christ our Lord.

39 *For civic officials*
We pray, O Lord, for all those in our community who are responsible for our welfare, health and security. May your Holy Spirit guide our councillors that they may have a care only for what will promote good government and bring the best for all who live in our town (village, city, etc.).

40 *For Christian unity*
Lord Jesus Christ we remember that you prayed that we may be one as you and our heavenly Father are one. We pray today for the unity of your church throughout the world. Help us, Lord, to play our part in healing the divisions which keep us from one another and which weaken our efforts to extend your kingdom of love in the world. Save us from all prejudice and give us an understanding of others' points of view so that your will may be done on earth as it is in Heaven.

41 *For parliament*
O Lord God almighty, guide, we pray, all to whom has been committed the government of this nation. We pray for politicians of all parties that they may be given special gifts of wisdom and understanding, of counsel and strength; that upholding what is right and following what is true, they may obey your holy will and fulfil your divine purpose.

42 *The new year*
O God our heavenly Father as we enter upon this new year we commit ourselves to your faithful care and keeping. Give us the grace to love you with all our hearts and a desire to love our

neighbours as ourselves. Throughout the year which lies ahead grant Lord that we may never turn aside from doing your will.

43 *For peace*
Almighty God we long for the day when nation shall not any more lift up sword against nation and when people everywhere will be able to live without fear but in security and peace. Help us in this time of strife to work and pray for peace in the world. Hasten, good Lord, that glorious day when your just and perfect will shall be embraced in every land.

44 *For a new term*
Grant Lord, at the beginning of this new term, that we may resolve always to do our best in our work and play. May we find happiness in work well done and in making the most of our opportunities of serving others and serving you, and may we never be distracted or diverted from our goal.

45 *New school year*
Be with us O Lord at the start of this new school year. Strengthen us to attain the goals that lie ahead of us. Give us the courage to go forward with confidence and a desire to make our best contribution to the life of our school.

46 *For friendship*
Teach us good Lord the value of true and lasting friendships which are based on equality and in which we all learn to give and take. May mutual respect and liking play their part and self-sacrifice and humour keep the relationships wholesome.

47 *A Christmas prayer*
Loving Father, we praise and thank you at Christmas time for your love to us in the gift of your son, Jesus Christ, who came to be our Saviour. May the love which came at Christmas be spread abroad throughout the world.

48 *For sports day*
Help us, O Lord, to be enthusiastic participants in our sport, understanding the true reason for our competitions. May we see the value of learning to play hard yet compete fairly and with good humour. May we use our sport to acquire fitness, skill, and so find fellowship and happiness.

49 *End of term*

We thank you, Lord, for the opportunities and successes of the term which is just ending. Forgive us for any failures and help us to learn from them. Grant us now enjoyable holidays in which we may know the pleasure of giving as well as receiving.

50 *School leavers*

We commend to your loving care and guidance, dear Father, those who are leaving school this term. Be with them as they go forward into their new life. May their path lead to success and self-fulfilment.

51 *The universe*

Help us, O Lord, to understand more about the universe in which we live. May we appreciate the beauty of the world you created. Make us always conscious of the needs of the people around us and the issues which should concern us.

52 *Spring*

Lord we give you thanks for the first flowers of spring and the new green shoots appearing on hedgerows and in our gardens. May we always show our gratitude to you Lord, for you are the giver of all good things.

53 *Summer*

At this time of light and warmth when the earth teems with life and movement, grant that we may observe the world of nature with gratitude and always pay our tribute to you, heavenly Father, the creator of all things.

54 *Autumn*

Father in Heaven as the days become shorter and we begin to think again of colder weather, help us to enjoy the mystery and glory of the autumn season. May we always be aware of the miracle of life which goes on around us. We thank you for your faithfulness in providing for all our needs.

55 *Winter*

Lord, open our eyes and make us aware of the beauty of nature even in winter time. We thank you for the splendour of the frost and the snow and for the certain promise that spring will not be long delayed.

56 *For endurance*

Give us courage, O Lord, to face the difficulties and pains of life as well as its successes and happiness. When we have to suffer, help us to endure our tribulations and trials with patience and fortitude. As you taught your disciples, help us to bear each other's burdens and may we remember that you have promised to be with us always.

57 *For those less fortunate*

Heavenly Father, help us always to be aware of the needs of people less fortunate than ourselves, the poor, the sick, the aged, the lonely, the homeless and all who need a helping hand. Show us how we can help to supply their needs and help them to know that there are people who care about them.

58 *A prayer for a time of disaster*

O God our loving Father, we pray today especially for all who are suffering as a result of the terrible disaster at . . . . We think of those who have been injured and those who have lost loved ones. Father we ask you to comfort and sustain them in their time of suffering and sorrow. We pray that you will give your strength and guidance to medical teams, relief workers and all who seek to bring help to the victims. In time we pray, Lord, that all who suffer may be given your peace.

Endings for prayers

1 . . . these our prayers we ask in and through the name of our Lord and Saviour Jesus Christ. Amen.
2 . . . this we ask in Jesus' name. Amen.
3 . . . this we ask for the sake of your Son Jesus Christ our Lord. Amen.
4 . . . Answer our prayers dear Father in accordance with your most holy will. Amen.

Graces

1 For food and all thy gifts of love
We give you thanks and praise,
Look down O Father from above
And bless us all our days.

2 For what we are about to receive
May the Lord may us truly thankful.

3 For food and fellowship
We thank you Heavenly Father.

4 Bless, O Lord, this food to our use
And ourselves in your service.

5 Be present at our table Lord
Be here and everywhere adored.
These children bless and grant that we
May dwell in paradise with thee. (John Wesley)

6 All good gifts around us
Are sent from Heaven above.
Then thank the Lord, O thank the Lord
For all his love. (Matthias Claudius)

7 (For younger children)
Thank you for the world so sweet,
Thank you for the food we eat,
Thank you for the birds that sing,
Thank you God for everything. (Edith Rutter Leatham)

Benedictions

1 The grace of the Lord Jesus Christ, the love of God and the fellowship of the Holy Spirit be with us all now and for evermore. Amen.

2 The peace of God which passes all understanding, keep your hearts and minds, through Jesus Christ our Lord. Amen.

3 Now unto the King, eternal, immortal, invisible, the only wise God, be honour and glory for ever and ever. Amen.

4 May grace, mercy and peace from God the Father, God the Son and God the Holy Spirit, be with us all, this day and always. Amen.

An assembly in case of bereavement

Today we have received sad news about one of our pupils. (*Here give the name of the pupil and details of the accident or illness.*) It is one of the facts of life that, unfortunately, accidents do happen and illnesses do occur, but this does not make tragedies any easier to bear or to understand. When one of our members is taken from us in the prime of life it is to be expected that we feel devastated. But what must his/her family and loved ones be feeling now? There seems little we can do or say at such a time but we hope that it will help them to know that . . . . had so many friends who wish to express their sympathy.

In the midst of life's tragedies and sorrows Christian people find that when they turn to God for help, he gives them an inner strength and courage to bear their sorrows. Listen, then, to these words of comfort and reassurance from the Bible:

Reading Psalm 46 God is our refuge and strength,
An ever present help in trouble.

Optional hymn at the beginning or end of the assembly
'He's got the whole world in his hand'
or
'The King of love my Shepherd is'

Prayer Today Heavenly Father we offer a special prayer for the family and friends of . . . . We ask you to be very near to them at this sad time, to comfort and sustain them in their sorrow, and that in time you will grant to them the peace which you alone can give. This our prayer we ask through Jesus Christ our Lord. Amen.

The Lord's Prayer

Traditional version

Our Father who art in Heaven
Hallowed be thy name.
Thy kingdom come,
Thy will be done
On earth as it is in Heaven.
Give us this day our daily bread,
And forgive us our trespasses,
As we forgive those who trespass against us.
And lead us not into temptation,
But deliver us from evil.
For thine is the kingdom,
The power and the glory,
For ever and ever. Amen.

Modern version (see New English Bible, *Matthew 6, 9–13)*

Our Father in Heaven
May your name be hallowed.
May your kingdom come
And your will be done
On earth as in Heaven.
Give us today our daily bread.
Forgive us the wrong we have done,
As we have forgiven those who have wronged us.
And do not bring us to the test,
But save us from evil. Amen.

Index of topics

Index of prayer topics

(Numbers refer to the prayers on pages 165–75)